GW01605810

TAPAS OF SAN SEBASTIAN

OVER 500 RECIPES FROM 150 CHEFS

Pedro Martín

PINTXOS OF DONOSTIA

First edition: june 2000
Second edition: july 2001

Portuetxe 88-bis
20018 Donostia
Tel: 943 310267 - Fax: 943 310216
ttarttalo@ttarttalo.com
www.ttarttalo.com

Photographs: Sara Santos, David Gil de Montes
Cover Photograph: Jesús Uriarte (Bar Bergara)
Translation: Iñaki Mendiguren *et al.*

We should like to thank Porcelanas del Bidasoa and Azulejos Larogei.
Design and Page layout: J. Félix Igartua and Imanol Tapia.
Photomechanics: Reproducciones Igara S.A.
Printed and Bound by Gráficas Lizarra, S. L.

I.S.B.N.: 84-8091-608-7
Legal Registration number: NA. 1.969-2001

FOREWORD

Juan Mari Arzak

Not long ago when my friend Pedro Martín asked me to write the forward for the first book about "Pintxos", snacks or tapas of Donostia-San Sebastian, I agreed to approach the readers of this book because I am a native of San Sebastian and because I am a chef. I think time will be the best judge and right now we can see and sample the development of our beloved "pintxos" in any corner of San Sebastian.

I have always thought that the "pintxos" are the most important thing we have. They are as important as our cuisine because they offer the most incredible quality and variety in small portions, they are freshly made and they do not exist anywhere else in the world.

"Pintxos" are an important phenomenon because in some way they represent the struggle against that dreadful fast food, which is doing us so much harm. I think that the young people and the not so young can have a fast, cheap meal in the form of "Pintxos".

This is a tremendous piece of work done by friend, Pedro Martín, (whom I call "Pedrito"). For many years now he has been working for this cause. He pioneered this type of book about "Pintxos", snacks or tapas, or miniature cuisine (whatever you like to call it), so I am delighted to see that this second book of this good friend of mine easily outclasses any other on the subject. I think the effort has been worthwhile and those of us of San Sebastian owe him a lot.

NOTES ON SOME INGREDIENTS AND UTENSILS

- **Peppers**: There are many types. The larger red peppers are called "Morrón". The smaller variety are known as "Piquillo" and these are generally used when preparing stuffed peppers. Both types are available in tins in which case they have already been roasted or grilled and had their skins removed. There are different varieties of green peppers. The smallest are the Gernika (or Padrón) ones.Then there is a larger variety, also grown locally, which is sometimes allowed to redden completely and sun-dried. These are referred to as "Choriceros" or dried spice peppers. The long thin "guindillas" or chili peppers are also grown in the Basque Country, some can be very hot and they are often pickled in vinegar.

- **Cod**: Salted cod is an important feature of Basque cuisine with its distinctive flavour. Before it can be used it has to have most of the salt removed. This is done by soaking the fish in water for 2 or 3 days, depending on the thickness of the pieces, and the water is changed a number of times.

- **Prawns**: There are mainly 2 types: the "Gamba" or smaller variety of prawn and the "Langostino" or large prawn.

- **Chorizo**: This is not unlike salami. It comes is different shapes and sizes and contains pork, salt and paprika, which gives it its distinctive red colour.

- **Earthenware dish (or "Cazuela de barro")**: These versatile, brown earthenware dishes can be seen in different sizes and are used for making sauces and cooking food gently, for which they are particulary suited, because of their thick bases.

INTRODUCTION

Pedro Martín

I could say that I have been the pioneer of this type of book, which has been very popular, but I never imagined this particular one would outclass the previous one by so much, etc. However, if I may be allowed, and as I do not like being pedantic, I should like to do this introduction my way.

I am very much aware of the great privilege I have had in being able to communicate with thousands of people through this new book, "Tapas or Pintxos of Donostia-San Sebastian". But in addition it had been especially gratifying being able to speak about such a marvellous subject as gastronomy.

It would be easy to talk about the marvels that appear in the book that you are holding, but you will be the best judge, and the fact is that, unlike other topics, we do not argue about the subject of good food, but rather we compare it, as my friend Miguel Gila would say, and if in addition we talk about the tapas of my country and his, then so much the better.

My aim or rather the aim of all of us (including over 150 chefs) who have been involved in producing this book, (I am very grateful to you for having a copy in your hands) is to enable you to recreate nearly 1000 images with your eyes. That way you will be able to surprise those around you by producing "miniature cuisine" (Juan M. Arzak) from the simplest to the most complicated of pintxos. For this purpose there are nearly 500 recipes with their ingredients and instructions on how to make them.

And to make things easier my friend and illustrious chef, Martín Berasategui, who received the Champerard Guide Best Basque Chef award for 1996, has written some pages explaining how to make the different sauces that appear in some of the recipes (mayonnaise, vinaigrette, cocktail sauce, etc.) and also the different ways of making them.

I should of course like to express my thanks to my colleagues who day after day and month after month have toiled to make this book a reality. Firstly my thanks not only to the 150 chefs and cooks and also to my friends Jaime Franco, Jesús Vicente, José de la Fuente or Alberto Altuna, led by Ibon Martín, all of whom acted as chauffeurs and "let's get going"(my friend Antonio Fraguas-Forges' words) which in this case meant "let's get going and get the pintxos, the tablecloth, etc.".

Here comes the best part. Turn the pages and enjoy our "Pintxos", "tapas" or "canapes", or whatever you like to call them, and if they will also help us as well as you to love the most beautiful city in the world even a little more , many thanks.

In the words of the master of humour, Miguel Gila, "Bon Appetit".

SAUCES AND BASES TO PREPARE THE PINTXOS

Martín Berasategi

PASTRY (PUFF)

Ingredients:

- *1kg flour*
- *200 g butter*
- *450 cc cold water*
- *24 g salt*
- *800 g butter*

Method:

Put the flour, salt and 200 g of butter in either a bowl or a kneading machine. If the pastry is to be made by hand, the butter should be softened with the finger tips and if by machine, then it should be hard and cut into cubes. Mix everything for half a minute and then add the water. Knead until you have a smooth dough.

Roll the dough into a ball and allow to stand in the fridge for half an hour.

Roll the butter into a rectangular shape without letting it get too soft.

After that roll the dough out into a rectangle slightly larger than the piece of butter.

Then put the butter in the shape of a diamond onto the dough and fold the dough as if it were a letter. Then roll it out and fold it six times. Allow it to stand for about 15 minutes every two folds.

Finally roll it out once more and freeze it so that it will not shrink when it is cut.

Then cut it into discs and mark a smaller circle in order to know where to position the pieces when the tart is made.

ALL-PURPOSE VINAIGRETTE

Ingredients:

- *100 cc of Módena balsam vinegar*
- *100 cc of sherry vinegar*
- *800 cc of 0.4° olive oil*
- *salt and pepper*

MILK MAYONNAISE

Method:

Make some mayonnaise using lemon juice instead of vinegar and with a quarter of its volume consisting of fresh milk. Season as necessary.

BÉCHAMEL SAUCE

This sauce can be used to make a light cream of vegetables (spinach works the best) or the typical croquettes. Everything depends on the thickness of the sauce.

This is how to make a light bechamel sauce.

Ingredients:

- *50 g of butter*
- *70 g of flour*
- *1 litre of milk*
- *grated nutmeg*
- *salt and pepper*

Method:

Melt the butter with the flour and allow it to cook a little, taking care the paste does not stick to the bottom of the pan.

Gradually add the very hot boiled milk. At first the paste will be a little thick but will become thinner as the milk is added. Allow to boil for a short time. The result should be a smooth, light cream. Add salt and pepper and nutmeg.

This sauce is the base for many dishes like fresh pasta, lasagne, spaghetti and for sauces in which different ingredients are added to this base.

TOMATO SAUCE

Ingredients:

- *1 kg ripe tomaoes*
- *3 onions*
- *1 leek*
- *2 cloves of garlic*
- *100 cc olive oil*

Method:

This sauce will serve as a base to make many sauces and dishes.

First select some very ripe tomatoes. Plum tomatoes are the best type.

Gently fry the vegetables in the oil and then add the tomatoes. Allow to cook slowly.

Then blend everything and allow to stand. Strain very carefully.

The sauce should be cooked for a long time on a low heat.

Add salt and sugar according to taste.

MAYONNAISE SAUCE

This is the most important feature of our cooking.

Thre are two ways of preparing it:

a) By machine (blender, electric mixer, electric beater etc....)

Ingredients:

- *1 egg*
- *300 cc of sunflower seed oil*
- *half the juice of a lemon*
- *salt*

Method:

Put all the ingredients together and beat. With some machines it takes 10 seconds. With other machines it takes a little longer, but not that much. The result should be a thick mixture with a mild taste.

Vinegar can be used instead of lemon juice, but lemon juice is preferable.

b) By hand:

Ingredients:

- *1 egg yolk*
- *150 cc of sunflower seed oil*
- *half the juice of one lemon*
- *salt*

Method:

With a hand whisk beat the egg yolk and gradually add the oil to it in a very fine stream.

This type of mayonnaise does not need as much oil as that made by machine.

The result is a little more yellow than and a little different from the one made by machine.

Both are equally good.

BATTER

Ingredients for 4 people:

- *eggs*
- *70g of sifted flour*
- *7 and 1/2 cl of lager beer*
- *salt*

Method: (5 minutes):

Separate the egg yolks from the egg whites.

Mix the yolks and flour in a bowl. Add a little salt.

Mix everything thoroughly and gradually add the beer.

Beat the egg whites stiffly in another bowl.

Gradually fold them into the other mixture with a wooden spatula and mix together very carefully.

HOMEMADE CREPES (PANCAKES)

Ingredients:

- *250 g of sifted flour*
- *100 g of powdered sugar*
- *a pinch of fine salt*
- *3 eggs*
- *3 and half decilitres of boiled milk*
- *flavour: orange blossom, rum, kirsch, or almond orgeat*

TARTARE SAUCE

To a litre of mayonnaise sauce add the following: 2 tablespoonfulls of capers and 6 chopped medium-sized gherkins plus the following herbs: parsley, chervil, estragon, chives, and if desired, some spoonfulls of Dijon mustard.

"ALI-OLI" SAUCE

Ingredients:

- *8 cloves of garlic*
- *2 egg yolks*
- *3 decilitres of oil*
- *a pinch of salt*
- *half a lemon*

Method:

Crush the garlic in a mortar; add the yolks and salt to the paste. Then add the oil drop by drop while at the same time continuing to stir with the pestle. Keep the sauce creamy by adding some drops of lemon juice from time to time (which is the acid ingredient of this sauce) and some tepid water.

PIMIENTO RELLENO
DE MARISCO

TARTALETA AINGERU

A I N G E R U

Padre Larroca nº 6 • Tel.: 943-27 19 44

TARTALETA AINGERU

AINGERU TARTLET

Ingredients: *Onion, green pepper, garlic, salt cod, mushroom, prawns, brandy, tomato sauce, cream, salt, pastry case, chopped parsley and grated cheese.*

Method: Heat the oil in a saucepan and gently fry half a chopped onion, a green pepper and two cloves of garlic. Then add the salt cod, mushroom and prawns. Cook everything on a low heat for 15 minutes. Then add half a glass of brandy, tomato sauce and cream. Serve hot garnished with parsley and grated cheese.

PIMIENTO RELLENO DE MARISCO

PEPPERS STUFFED WITH SEAFOOD

Ingredients: *"Piquillo" red peppers, spider crab, prawns, flour, salt and the stock in which the prawns have been boiled. For the sauce: onion, green pepper, garlic, tomato, cream and brandy.*

Ingredients: Put a little butter in a saucepan to heat, add the chopped spider crab and prawns. Season and mix with a little flour and prawn stock and cook. Leave to cool and then stuff the peppers. Serve with cocktail sauce.

REVUELTO DE AJOS FRESCOS CON GAMBAS

FRESH GARLIC SHOOTS AND PRAWN SCRAMBLED EGG

Ingredients: *Fresh garlic shoots, prawns, eggs, salt and garlic*

Method: Peel and chop the raw prawns and put in a frying pan with oil and garlic. When the garlic and prawns have browned slightly, add the beaten egg with the fresh garlic. Stir a little ensuring that the mixture doesn't get too dry.

AL PEQUEÑO
SALMÓN
AMARA ZAHARRA

AL PEQUEÑO

Autonomía nº 1 • Tel.: 943-45 65 42

A L P E Q U E Ñ O

AL PEQUEÑO

Ingredients: *Anchovies in oil, peppers, garlic and bread.*

Method: Put the anchovies on the bread and the peppers on top. Cover with chopped garlic.

S A L M Ó N

SALMON

Ingredients: *Bread, smoked salmon and hard-boiled egg.*

Method: Put a slice of smoked salmon on the piece of bread, then a slice of hard- boiled egg. Garnish with grated egg.

A M A R A Z A H A R R A

AMARA ZAHARRA

Ingredients: *Hard-boiled egg, prawn, mayonnaise and olives.*

Method: Put all the ingredients on to a cocktail stick and cover with mayonnaise. Garnish with a small piece of pepper, as in the photograph.

PIMIENTO CON ANCHOA

ENSALADA DE PIMIENTOS Y JAMÓN

PULPO A LA VINAGRETA

A L C A L D E

Mayor nº 19 • Tel.: 943-42 62 16/42 80 90

P I M I E N T O   C O N   A N C H O A

PEPPER WITH ANCHOVY

Ingredients: *"Piquillo" red peppers and anchovies.*

Method: Chop the peppers and put them on a slice of toasted bread. Put two anchovies on the peppers and garnish with grated white of hard-boiled egg. Add some colour with a pinch of chopped parsley.

E N S A L A D A   D E   P I M I E N T O S   Y   J A M Ó N

PEPPER AND HAM SALAD

Ingredients: *Red pepper, green pepper, boiled ham, Emmental cheese and mayonnaise.*

Method: Chop up the peppers, ham and cheese. Mix the ingredients with mayonnaise and put on a slice of bread. Decorate with a pinch of hot paprika.

P U L P O   A   L A   V I N A G R E T A

OCTOPUS WITH VINAIGRETTE

Ingredients: *Octopus, red pepper, green pepper, onion, vinegar, oil and salt.*

Method: Boil the octopus and cut into pieces. Put the pieces on cocktail sticks and pour over the vinaigrette sauce, made with the remaining ingredients.

BAHÍA

LARRAMENDI

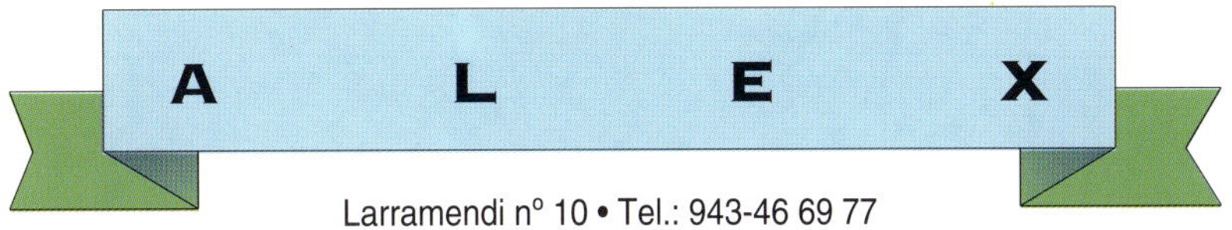

A L E X

Larramendi nº 10 • Tel.: 943-46 69 77

B A H Í A

BAHIA

Ingredients: *Toasted bread, boiled ham, smoked salmon, crab sticks and mayonnaise.*

Method: Spread a little mayonnaise on a slice of toasted bread, cover it with the ham and on top of that the slice of smoked salmon. Finally add the cut-up crab sticks mixed with mayonnaise.

L A R R A M E N D I

LARRAMENDI

Ingredients: *Sliced bread, large prawns, lettuce or hard-boiled egg and cocktail sauce.*

Method: Cut the sliced bread into circles and spread with mayonnaise. Put the large prawns on top of the bread to form a circle. In the centre put some finely sliced lettuce or hard-boiled egg, and decorate with some cocktail sauce.

A L E X

ALEX

Ingredients: *Bread, anchovy and hard-boiled egg.*

Method: On a slice of bread put some anchovies in the shape of a small square. Fill the centre with finely chopped hard-boiled egg white. Serve with some drops of Tabasco sauce or Worcester sauce.

MILHOJAS DE FOIE

BRANDADA DE BACALAO

TARTALETA DE LECHERITAS

ALOÑA BERRI

Berminghan nº 24 • Tel.: 943-29 08 18

MILHOJAS DE FOIE

LIVER PATE MILLE FEUILLE

Ingredients: *Liver pâté, sliced potato, kiwi, plums and toasted bread.*

Method: This is a mille feuille consisting of slices of boiled potato, liver pâté , a slice of kiwi and the plums. All this is then put onto a piece of toasted bread.

BRANDADA DE BACALAO

COD "BRANDADA"

Ingredients: *Salt cod, garlic, quails' eggs, Hollandaise sauce and pastry case.*

Method: Gently fry the cod with four cloves of garlic in olive oil. After that remove the skin and bones, and then flake. Put the cod in the pastry case. Put the quails' eggs on top and cover with the Hollandaise sauce.

TARTALETA DE LECHERITAS

SWEETBREAD TARTLETS

Ingredients: *Calves' sweetbreads, shallot, dry sherry, tomato sauce, brandy, fresh pasta, parsley and pastry case.*

Method: Boil the sweet breads for about 5 minutes, let them cool and cut them into pieces. Fry the finely chopped shallot, add the sweetbreads and when hot put in the brandy and flambé everything. Add the tomato sauce and put the mixture into a pastry case. Finally cover with fresh pasta and parsley.

CALABACÍN
CON AJOARRIERO

BERENJENAS
CON CHIPIRÓN

CALABACÍN CON AJOARRIERO

COURGETTE WITH "AJOARRIERO"

Ingredients: *I courgette, 1 onion, 1 green pepper, 200 ml of tomato sauce, 250 grammes of salt cod and 3 dried spice peppers.*

Method: Cut the courgette and boil it for two minutes. Drain. Prepare some lightly fried finely chopped onion and green pepper. Add the flaked cod, and toss everything in the oil. Then add the tomato sauce and flesh of the spice peppers. Allow everything to cook. Then fill the courgettes with this mixture or "ajoarriero" and garnish to taste.

BERENJENAS CON CHIPIRÓN

AUBERGINES WITH SQUID

Ingredients: *Aubergines, onion, green pepper, garlic, tomato sauce, olive oil and white wine.*

Method: Dice the aubergines. Chop the onion, pepper and garlic and sauté with the aubergines and tomatoes. Cook this mixture until it thickens. Clean the squid and toss them in the frying pan with the oil and white wine.

Serve as shown in the photograph.

ROLLITO DE SALMÓN AHUMADO

SMOKED SALMON ROLL

Ingredients: *Smoked salmon, fresh salmon, lemon juice, mayonnaise, mustard, curly lettuce, pepper and dill.*

Method: Cook the fresh salmon with olive oil, lemon juice, salt, pepper and dill. Fill the smoked salmon with the fresh salmon and mayonnaise with mustard. Garnish with curly lettuce.

FOIE AL OPORTO

SÁBANA DE ENDIBIA Y CONFIT

ENSALADA DE TXANGURRO Y MARISCO

ALOTZA

Fermín Calbetón nº 7 • Tel.: 943-42 07 82

FOIE AL OPORTO

LIVER WITH PORT

Ingredients: *Goose liver, port, pippin apple, toasted bread, butter and red Italian chicory or "radicchio" cut into julienne strips.*

Method: Toast the bread and cut it into a circle with a pastry cutter. Put the stewed apple on the circle of toast. Cut a slice of goose liver, sprinkle with the port, season, and then fry it. Put it on the apple. Serve with two balls of butter and the red Italian chicory cut into julienne strips.

SÁBANA DE ENDIBIA Y CONFIT

BELGIAN ENDIVES WITH DUCK CONFIT

Ingredients: *Belgian endive, duck "confit", olive oil, raspberry vinegar, salt and chervil.*

Method: Heat a portion of duck "confit" and put it on an endive leaf. Make a vinaigrette with pure olive oil and raspberry vinegar. Sprinkle over the endive and the duck, and garnish with chervil.

ENSALADA DE TXANGURRO Y MARISCO

SPIDER CRAB AND SEAFOOD SALAD

Ingredients: *Lettuce hearts from Tudela, spider crab, prawns, small Norway lobsters, mayonnaise, half an onion, a few drops of Tabasco sauce.*

Method: Chop the lettuce hearts and onion. Flake the spider crab and chop the prawns and Norway lobsters, which have been boiled beforehand. Mix all the ingredients with the mayonnaise and tabasco sauce. Serve in a pastry case.

PINTXO DE
SALMÓN

PINTXO DE
LANGOSTINOS

ALTO AQUÍ

San Bartolomé nº 11 • Tel.: 943-45 01 01

PINTXO DE ANCHOA

ANCHOVY "PINTXO" OR CANAPE

Ingredients: *4 slices of French bread, 4 anchovies, 4 pieces of fried red pepper with the skin removed, 4 pieces of fried green pepper with the skin removed, cocktail sauce, grated hard-boiled egg white and green olives without stones.*

Method: To make the cocktail sauce add tomato ketchup, a teaspoonful of mustard, some drops of Worcester sauce, a little brandy and some drops of Tabasco sauce to the mayonnaise. To make the canapé, toast the bread, spread the cocktail sauce on it, on one side of each slice put the piece of red pepper and on the other the piece of green pepper. Put the anchovy on top, then the grated hard-boiled egg white and the olive.

PINTXO DE SALMÓN

SALMON "PINTXO"

Ingredients: *Sliced bread, tuna fish, cocktail sauce, salmon and onion.*

Method: Cut the sliced bread into small squares. Cover with a layer of cocktail sauce, and put a layer of tuna fish mixed with cocktail sauce on top. Cover with another slice and spread again wth the cocktail sauce. Finally put a slice of smoked salmon and some pieces of onion on top.

PINTXO DE LANGOSTINOS

LARGE PRAWN "PINTXO"

Ingredients: *French bread, hard-boiled egg, large prawns (boiled), crab sticks, chopped onion and cocktail sauce.*

Method: Mix all the ingredients together. Put a little cocktail sauce over everything and spread on the slice of bread.

PINTXO DE BACALAO

BACALAO AJOARRIERO

PIMIENTOS RELLENOS DE BACALAO

PINTXO DE BACALAO

SALT COD "PINTXO" OR CANAPE

Ingredients: *Fillets of cod, green pepper, onion flour and egg.*

Method: Remove the salt from the cod fillets. Dip in flour and egg and fry in hot olive oil. On top of the cod put some strips of gently fried onion and some strips of green pepper, which have been fried beforehand and have had the skin removed.

BACALAO AJOARRIERO

COD "AJOARRIERO"

Ingredients: *Flaked cod fillets, spring onions, tomato sauce and potatoes.*

Method: Remove the salt from the cod, chop the spring onions and garlic and gently fry in olive oil in a frying pan. When the onions and garlic are soft, add the cod and let it cook gently. When it is ready add the tomato sauce, bring to the boil and move away from the heat. Then fry the potatoes in very thin strips in olive oil, drain and add them to the cod. All this is then brought to the boil once again before it is ready to eat.

PIMIENTOS RELLENOS DE BACALAO

PEPPERS STUFFED WITH COD

Ingredients: *"Piquillo" peppers, flaked cod fillets, green peppers, spring onions, flour, milk, tomato sauce, brandy and black pepper.*

Method: Remove the salt from the cod and gently fry the finely chopped onions and green peppers in olive oil in a frying pan. Add the flaked cod and then a little flour and milk to make a light béchamel sauce. Fill the "piquillo" peppers with the sauce and put to one side. To make the sauce gently fry some spring onions in olive oil and add a glass of good brandy, some black pepper and tomato sauce. Using a blender turn all this into a smooth sauce.

CHAMPIS

PATATA RELLENA

MUSLOS DE POLLO

ALTUNA

San Martin • Tel.: 943-46 73 21

CHAMPIÑÓNES

MUSHROOMS

Ingredients: *Button mushrooms, onion, garlic, parsley, black pepper and a little cayenne pepper.*

Method: Fry the onion without letting it brown. Crush the garlic, parsley and cayenne pepper and mix them with the onion and mushrooms, which have been washed. Fry everything together in the oil and allow to stand before serving.

PATATA RELLENA

STUFFED POTATO

Ingredients: *Potatoes, mince meat, egg and bread-crumbs.*

Method: Cut the potatoes into discs and fry. Between one disc and another put a little mince meat cooked according to taste. Dip in egg and breadcrumbs and fry in very hot oil.

MUSLOS DE POLLO

CHICKEN DRUMSTICKS

Ingredients: *Chicken drumsticks, leek, carrot, tomato, egg and breadcrumbs.*

Method: Boil the drumsticks with the leek, carrot and tomato. When cooked, remove and drain. Fry each drumstick in egg and breadcrumbs and serve.

FRITOS VARIADOS

CREPES DE CHIPIRON

PINTXOS DE LASAGNA

ANDRA MARI

Zabaleta • Tel.: 943-28 81 91

FRITOS VARIADOS

MIXED CROQUETTES

Ingredients: *I litre of milk for about 35 croquettes, 8 dessertpoonfulls of flour, half a litre of oil, a knob of butter and a pinch of salt. All this is suitable for prawn, cheese, egg, or ham croquettes.*

Method: Heat the oil and butter in a saucepan and add the flour. Heat and stir with a wooden spoon. Add the milk gradually until the mixture thickens. Then put in one of the ingredients (prawns, cheese, egg or ham in small pieces). Allow the mixture to cool. Then cut the mixture and work the ingredients into a circular or oval shape. Then dip them in flour, egg and breadcrumbs and fry.

CRÊPES DE CHIPIRÓN

SQUID PANCAKES

Ingredients: *For 8 pancakes: 600 g of small, cleaned squid, 1 onion, 1 clove of garlic, 50 ml of oil and a pinch of salt.*

Method: Brown the onion and fry the squid, which has been minced. When it has cooked sufficiently add a glass of white wine, allow to boil a little more and drain. Roll the mixture in the pancakes. Put to heat in a microwave or conventional oven and cover with a layer of squid sauce.

PINTXOS DE LASAGNA

LASAGNE PINTXO

Ingredients: *1 pastry case of either puff or short pastry, 100 g of chopped onion, 250 g of mince meat, 100 g of sliced button mushrooms, 300 g of Italian pasta, 100 g of butter, 250 g of flour, 200 g of grated cheese and half a glass of oil.*

Method: Fry the onion in a saucepan with the oil and butter. Add the mince before the onion browns. Cook and then add the mushroom. Add half of the white sauce which has been prepared beforehand and half the pasta, which has also been boiled beforehand. Stir the mixture and spoon into the pastry case. Put the rest of the white sauce and pasta on top and also the grated cheese. Cook in the oven for 15 minutes at a temperature of 200°C.

CALAMARES
FRITOS

PINTXOS DE
KRABARROKA

BACALAO
ANDRA MARI

CALAMARES FRITOS

FRIED SQUID

Ingredients: *For 8 portions: 2 kilos of fresh squid and flour.*

Method: Clean the squid and cut into rings. Coat with flour and shake off the excess flour. Fry at a temperature of 250° and when the rings are brown, remove and serve with a slice of lemon.

PINTXOS DE KRABARROKA

ROCKFISH CANAPES

Ingredients: *1 and 1/4 kilos of rockfish, half a litre of cream, half a tin of tomato sauce and 4 beaten eggs.*

Method: Boil the rockfish and remove the skin and bones. Put all the flaked fish into a bowl and add the cream, the tomato and the beaten eggs. Mix together and put in a mould lined with butter and breadcrumbs. Allow it to cool a little in the fridge. Spread the mixture evenly in the mould and cook in the oven bain marie for 1 hour at a temperature of 225°.

BACALAO ANDRA MARI

ANDRA MARI COD

Ingredients: *8 pieces of cod, 200 g of green pepper, 200 g of onion cut into julienne strips prepared beforehand, a tin of tomato sauce.*

Method: Put 50 ml of oil, the green pepper and the onion into a pan. Put the pieces of cod on top and move the pan back and forth so that the sauce thickens well. Add the tomato and continue moving the pan to thicken the sauce further. The cod does not take long to cook, but this will depend on the thickness of the pieces.

PIQUILLO Y
GERNIKAS

PASTEL DE
MERLUZA

A N I C E T O

Eustasio Amilibia nº 7 • Tel.: 943-45 21 29

P I Q U I L L O   Y   G E R N I K A S

"PIQUILLO" AND GERNIKA PEPPERS

Ingredients: *3 "piquillo" peppers, 3 local green peppers, hard-boiled egg, crab sticks and mayonnaise.*

Method: Mix the crab sticks and mayonnaise. Stuff the peppers with this mixture. Arrange on a plate with alternating colours and garnish with the hard-boiled egg.

H O J A L D R E   D E   G A M B A S

PRAWNS IN PASTRY

Ingredients: *Puff pastry, 3 prawns, leeks, onion, tomato and brandy.*

Method: Make a sauce with the chopped prawns, onion, leek, brandy and tomato in a frying pan. Mince everything and fill the pastry with this sauce.

P A S T E L   D E   M E R L U Z A

HAKE TART

Ingredients: *500 g of hake, 6 eggs, tomato, cream, mayonnaise and parsley.*

Method: First boil the fish, flake it and mix it with the eggs, cream and tomato. Put the mixture in a mould lined with butter. Cook in the oven bain marie for an hour at medium heat. When it is cooked, cut it into slices and garnish with the mayonnaise, hard-boiled egg and parsley.

TARTALETA DE FOIE

HOJALDRE DE PISTO CON GAMBAS

RIOJANITO

ANTONIO

Bergara nº 3 • Tel.: 943-42 98 15

TARTALETA DE FOIE

LIVER PATE TARTLETS

Ingredients: *Pastry case, 2 slices of courgette, liver pâté, egg, flour and breadcrumbs.*

Method: Gently fry two slices of courgette coated in flour and egg. When they are fried fill them with liver paté and coat them once again, this time in egg and breadcrumbs. Make a sauce with a lot of onion, a little oil, salt, sugar and stock cube. Cook this gently and when it is soft, add a little orange juice and white wine. Then blend the sauce and put some on the pastry case containing the stuffed courgette. Decorate according to taste.

HOJALDRE DE PISTO CON GAMBAS

RATATOUILLE AND PRAWNS IN PASTRY

Ingredients: *Pastry tartlet, courgette, prawns, onion, green pepper and garlic.*

Method: In a saucepan brown the onion with a clove of garlic and green pepper. When they are soft add the diced courgette and cook gently. When everything is very soft add the prawns which have been fried beforehand. Finally put this ratatouille mixture in the tartlet.

RIOJANITO

RIOJANITO

Ingredients: *Pastry case, minced "chorizo" sausage and quail's egg.*

Method: You have to get hold of a good Riojan minced chorizo sausage. You then fry it and put it in a tartlet with a fried quail's egg on top.

TXOPITOS

PINTXO FRÍO
DE QUESO
DE BURGOS

ANCHOA EN SALAZÓN

SALTY ANCHOVIES

Ingredients: *A slice of freshly toasted bread, a salty anchovy from the Bay of Biscay, a small piece of hot chili pepper, and some strips of green pepper, which have been gently cooked in oil and then allowed to soak in white wine with a little garlic.*

Method: Put the hot chili pepper, the anchovy and the green peppers on the slice of toast.

TXOPITOS

BABY SQUID

Ingredients: *Baby squid, small green"Padrón" peppers, flour and salt.*

Method: Clean the baby squid, coat in flour and put some salt on them. Fry on a high heat together with the green peppers.

PINTXO FRÍO DE QUESO DE BURGOS

FRIED BURGOS CHEESE PINTXO

Ingredients: *A slice of bread, gently cooked green peppers, two anchovies in oil, anchovy paste and Burgos cheese (similar to Ricotta cheese).*

Method: Put a little home-made anchovy paste on a slice of bread. Then put a thin slice of cooked green pepper and the cheese. On top of that put two anchovies and a slice of olive.

PIMIENTO DEL PIQUILLO RELLENO

BONITO ENCEBOLLADO CON ANCHOA

PINCHO DE ROQUEFORT CON NUECES

ARALAR

Puerto nº 10 • Tel.: 943-42 63 78

PIMIENTO DEL PIQUILLO RELLENO

STUFFED "PIQUILLO" PEPPER

Ingredients: *"Piquillo" peppers from Mendavia, pickled tuna fish, onion, mayonnaise, olive oil, vinegar and salt.*

Method: Flake the tuna and chop the onion finely. Mix with the mayonnaise and add a little tartare sauce. Stuff the peppers with this mixture and dress with olive oil and salt.

BONITO ENCEBOLLADO CON ANCHOA

TUNA FISH WITH ONION AND ANCHOVY

Ingredients: *Pickled tuna fish, onion, anchovy in oil and capers.*

Method: Mix the flaked tuna and very finely chopped onion with the mayonnaise. Add a little vinegar and some capers. Spread the mixture onto a slice of bread and garnish with an anchovy.

PINCHO DE ROQUEFORT CON NUECES

ROQUEFORT AND WALNUT PINTXO

Ingredients: *Roquefort cheese, cream, Scandinavian crispbread and walnuts.*

Method: Make a spread with the cream and the cheese, put it on the bread and decorate with the walnuts.

BACALAO AL
AJOARRIERO

PUDÍN DE
MERLUZA Y
GAMBA

BACALAO AL AJOARRIERO

COD WITH "AJOARRIERO"

Ingredients: *Cod, garlic, green pepper, red pepper, onion, olive oil, potato and hot cayenne pepper.*

Method: Gently fry the finely chopped onion, garlic and pepper in the oil. When it is soft add the cod which has already been flaked and had the salt removed. Finally add the pepper and remove from the heat. A small amount of potato is added to the canape when it is put on a piece of bread.

LECHERITA DE CORDERO DE LECHE

BABY LAMB SWEETBREADS

Ingredients: *Lamb sweetbreads, salt, egg, garlic, parsley, olive oil and breadcrumbs.*

Method: Allow the sweetbreads to soak in the beaten egg with salt, garlic and parsely. Then dip in breadcrumbs and fry in olive oil.

PUDÍN DE MERLUZA Y GAMBA

PRAWN AND HAKE PUDDING

Ingredients: *Hake, cream, tomato sauce, cognac, white pepper, eggs, sliced bread and one prawn per canapé.*

Method: Boil the hake. Beat the eggs with the cream and a little tomato sauce. When the hake is cool, break it up into flakes, and mix with the eggs, etc. Season and cook in the oven in a mould bain marie. When the pudding is cool, turn it out and put slices of it on to the sliced bread. Decorate with a squirt of mayonnaise and a boiled, peeled prawn.

FOIE POCHADO
AL ARMAGNAC

CAZUELA DE
AHUMADOS

A R A N A

José Arana nº 2 • Tel.: 943-28 49 26

F O I E P O C H A D O A L A R M A G N A C

LIVER POACHED IN ARMAGNAC

Ingredients: *A goose liver, or if not available, a duck liver, goose fat, armagnac and toasted bread.*

Method: Marinade the liver in the armagnac for three hours and and turn it over from time to time. Then drain and season. Grease an oval earthenware dish with the goose fat and gently cook the liver in it on a low heat for 20 minutes continually turning it over. When cold, cut into thin slices and put on a slice of toasted bread.

C A Z U E L A D E A H U M A D O S

SMOKED FISH PLATTER

Ingredients: *Smoked slamon, smoked anchovies, large boiled prawns, cocktail sauce, hard-boiled egg, mayonnaise, vinaigrette and toasted bread.*

Method: Cover each slice of toasted bread with finely chopped hard-boiled egg. On top of that put a piece of salmon, an anchovy and a large prawn. Garnish with cocktail sauce and vinaigrette.

E N S A L A D A D E L A N G O S T A

LARGE LOBSTER SALAD

Ingredients: *Boiled lobster tail, soya bean sprouts, celery, button mushrooms, red pepper, palm heart, parsley, oil, lemon and bread.*

Method: Slice the lobster tail. Prepare a salad with the above ingredients. Put two slices of lobster on a slice of bread and then some of the salad on top. Garnish according to taste.

SALPICÓN DE
MARISCO
ATÚN
YONCAR
PASTEL DE
PESCADO

ARBELAIZKO J&V

José María Salaberría • Tel.: 943-45 68 73

SALPICÓN DE MARISCO

SEAFOOD COCKTAIL

Ingredients: *Hake fillets, eggs, large prawns, small prawns, salt, oil and mayonnaise.*

Method: Boil the fish, seafood and eggs. Flake the fish and remove the bones and skin. Peel the large and small prawns. Chop some of them to mix with the fish and keep a few for decorating the canapes. Chop up the hard-boiled egg, season and mix with the mayonnaise. Put the mixture on a slice of bread and garnish with the small prawns.

ATÚN YONCAR

YONCAR TUNA FISH

Ingredients: *Tuna fish in oil, thin green peppers in vinegar, onion, anchovies in oil and mayonnaise.*

Method: Finely chop the thin green peppers and onion. Mix them with the tuna fish and the mayonnaise. Spread the mixture onto a slice of bread and garnish with an anchovy.

PASTEL DE PESCADO

FISH CAKE

Ingredients: *Oil, salt, flour, milk, butter, onion, fish, tomato sauce and mayonnaise.*

Method: Fry the onion in a spoonful of oil, add a knob of butter, 2 spoonfulls of flour, and a glass of milk. Make a thick white (bechamel) sauce, add the boiled fish. Give the mixture a touch of colour with the tomato sauce and allow to cool. Spread the mixture onto a slice of bread and garnish with mayonnaise.

PIMIENTOS RELLENOS DE BACALAO

PUDÍN DE TXANGURRO

SEPIA

ARDANDEGI

Reyes Católicos nº 7 • Tel.: 943 46 74 77

PIMIENTOS RELLENOS DE BACALAO

PEPPERS STUFFED WITH COD

Ingredients: *Cod, "piquillo" peppers, onion, green pepper, milk, flour and butter.*

Method: Gently fry the cod with the onion and green pepper. Make a white (bechamel) sauce and add it. Stuff the peppers with this mixture.

PUDÍN DE TXANGURRO

SPIDER CRAB PUDDING

Ingredients: *Leeks, brandy, cream, tomato, eggs, white pepper, salt and spider crab.*

Method: Chop up all the ingredients including the spider crab. Grease a mould with some butter. Put the mixture in the mould and cook in the oven bain marie. When it is ready, garnish with mayonnaise.

SEPIA

CUTTLEFISH

Ingredients: *4 small cuttlefish, very finely chopped garlic, very finely chopped parsley, vinegar, olive oil and salt.*

Method: Grill the cuttlefish with oil and salt. When they have browned, remove from the heat and pour vinaigrette over them.

PINTXO
PRIMAVERA
ANCHOAS EN
VINAGRETA
PIMIENTOS
DEL
PIQUILLO

PINTXO PRIMAVERA

SPRING CANAPE

Ingredients: *Eggs, boiled ham, mayonnaise, lettuce cut into julienne strips, sliced bread and red pepper.*

Method: Mix the chopped egg and ham together with the mayonnaise and spread the mixture onto a piece of sliced bread, which has been toasted. Cover with another slice of toasted bread and decorate with the lettuce, a little mayonnaise, grated hard-boiled egg and a little chopped pepper.

ANCHOAS EN VINAGRETA

ANCHOVIES IN VINAIGRETTE

Ingredients: *Anchovies, salt, vinegar, oil, water and parsley.*

Method: Steep the anchovies for a couple of hours in a bowl of vinegar, water and salt. Then remove them from the liquid and put them in another bowl of oil, garlic and parsley.

PIMIENTOS DEL PIQUILLO

"PIQUILLO" PEPPERS

Ingredients: *"Piquillo" peppers, olive oil, chopped garlic, salt and anchovies.*

Method: Cut the peppers into thin strips and add olive oil, sliced garlic and salt. Arrange on slices of toasted bread and garnish with anchovies in oil.

TARTALETAS

CAPRICHO

ASCENSIO

Felipe IV nº 4 • Tel.: 943-45 31 29

TARTALETAS

TARTLETS

Ingredients: *Potato, carrot, peas, hard-boiled egg, mayonnaise, prawns, pastry, lettuce and roquefort cheese.*

Method: Make a Russian salad with the potato, carrot, peas, mayonnaise and hard-boiled egg. Make tartlets with the pastry. Put some chopped lettuce in the bottom of each one and fill with the Russian salad. Decorate some of the tartlets with mayonnaise and prawns and others with mayonnaise and roquefort cheese.

GAMBAS CON BECHAMEL

PRAWNS WITH BECHAMEL SAUCE

Ingredients: *Flour, butter, milk, salt, garlic, parsley, prawns and egg.*

Method: Make a light bechamel sauce and add a little garlic and parsley to it. Put 2 prawns on to a cocktail stick, coat them with the bechamel sauce, dip them in flour and then egg and fry them in deep oil.

CAPRICHO

CAPRICE

Ingredients: *Bread, "Piquillo" peppers from Lodosa, anchovies in oil, hard-boiled egg, mayonnaise and cocktail sauce.*

Method: Cut a piece of bread. Put a pepper and two anchovy fillets on it. Then put a slice of hard-boiled egg on top of that and decorate with the two sauces.

MORROS
BACALAO
PASTEL DE
PESCADO

ASTELENA

Iñigo nº 1 • Tel.: 943-42 62 75

MORROS

CALVES' MUZZLES

Ingredients: *Calves' muzzles, flour, onion , white wine and beef stock cube for the sauce.*

Method: Boil the muzzles and when they are done fry them in flour and beaten egg. Make a game sauce with the flour, onion, white wine and stock. Cook the muzzles in the sauce for 20 minutes.

BACALAO

COD

Ingredients: *Cod, onion, green pepper, chili pepper and oil.*

Method: When the salt has been removed from the cod, cut the cod into squares. Put plenty of oil in a pan and fry the onion cut into julienne strips, green pepper and chili pepper. Then add the cod and cook it for 10 minutes.

PASTEL DE PESCADO

FISH CAKE

Ingredients: *Any kind of white fish, egg and tomato.*

Method: Boil the fish and then flake it. Break 6 eggs into a separate bowl together with a kilo of cooked tomato for each kilo of fish. Beat the mixture well and mix with the flaked fish. Grease a mould with butter and put the mixture into it. Bake in the oven bain marie for half an hour per kilo of fish plus a further half an hour.

CHAMPI ATARI

PRIMAVERA

GERNIKA

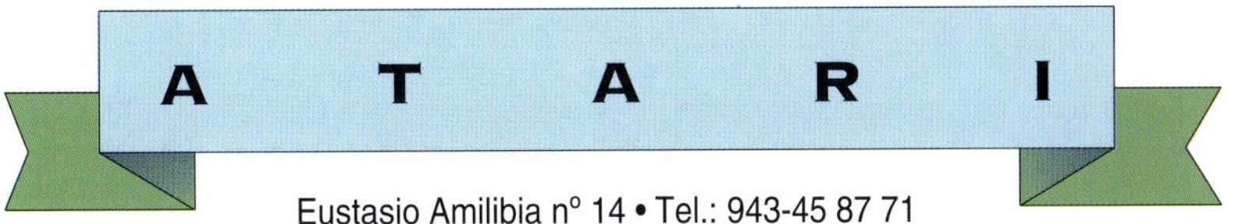

ATARI

Eustasio Amilibia nº 14 • Tel.: 943-45 87 71

PRIMAVERA

SPRING

Ingredients: *Lettuce, crab sticks, mayonnaise, bread, boiled prawns.*

Method: Wash the lettuce and cut into very fine julienne strips. Cut the crab sticks into small pieces and mix with the lettuce and 2 spoonfulls of mayonnaise. Put the mixture on to a piece of bread and a prawn on top of it.

CHAMPI ATARI

ATARI MUSHROOMS

Ingredients: *Large button mushrooms, prawns, salt, garlic, parsley, olive oil and hot spicy sauce.*

Method: Wash and dry the mushrooms and remove the stalk. Take a cocktail stick and spear a mushroom on to one end and a prawn onto the other. Grill for 2 minutes on each side. Sprinkle with a mixture of finely chopped garlic, parsley ,hot sauce and olive oil.

GERNIKA

GERNIKA

Ingredients: *Gernika peppers, red pepper, hard-boiled egg, anchovies, onion and toasted bread.*

Method: Fry the Gernika peppers and slice them down the middle. Chop one of the halves and mix it with the finely chopped onion and finely chopped red pepper. Spear the other half of the pepper onto the toasted bread and put a slice of hard-boiled egg on top. Then put the chopped pepper and onion mixture on top of the egg and put the anchovies in oil on each side of the bread.

BACALAO AUKERA

CALAMARES

CHATKA CON
SALMÓN

AUKERA

Felipe IV nº 3 • Tel.: 943-45 91 38

BACALAO AUKERA

AUKERA COD

Ingredients: *Olive oil, onion, green pepper and wedges of cod*

Method: Fry the onion and pepper. Coat the cod in flour and fry for 3 minutes. Cover the cod with the fried onion and pepper and serve hot.

CALAMARES

SQUID

Ingredients: *Fresh squid, flour and salt.*

Method: Clean the squid thoroughly and cut into pieces. Coat in flour and fry for 2 minutes. Season and serve hot.

CHATKA CON SALMÓN

CRAB STICKS WITH SALMON

Ingredients: *Crab sticks, smoked salmon, anchovies in oil, caviar, mayonnaise, onion and parsley.*

Method: Finely chop the onion and add a little finely chopped parsley. Cut up the crab sticks and mix them with the onion, parsley and mayonnaise. You can decorate this with salmon, anchovy and caviar.

PIMIENTOS RELLENOS

MEJILLONES RELLENOS

VEGETAL

BARTOLO

Fermin Calbetón nº 38 • Tel.: 943-42 17 43

PIMIENTOS RELLENOS

STUFFED PEPPERS

Ingredients: *"Piquillo" peppers, green pepper, tuna fish, chili pepper, mayonnaise, onion and bread.*

Method: Make the stuffing with the red and green pepper, tuna, chili pepper and mayonnaise and fill the peppers with it. Put each one on a piece of bread and garnish with a little vinaigrette.

MEJILLONES RELLENOS

STUFFED MUSSELS

Ingredients: *Red and green peppers, mussels, onion, garlic, parsley, white pepper, tomato, tabasco sauce, hard-boiled egg, bechamel sauce, breadcrumbs and flour.*

Method: Cook the vegetables and add the tomato sauce and finely chopped egg and mussels. Add salt, pepper and tabasco sauce to taste. When the mixture has cooled, fill the mussel shells and cover with the white sauce. Finally dip into beaten egg and breadcrumbs and fry.

VEGETAL

VEGETABLE PINTXO

Ingredients: *Bread, lettuce, "piquillo" pepper, egg, mayonnaise and anchovy in oil.*

Method: Put a thin layer of lettuce on the bread to form a base. Cut the hard-boiled egg in half and cut a small piece of each half to use as a cover. Fill the egg with a slice of pepper, put the egg cover on top and decorate with mayonnaise and an anchovy.

PIMIENTO RELLENO DE BACALAO

MEJILLÓN RELLENO

BASARRI

Fermin Calbetón nº 17 • Tel.: 943-42 58 53

PIMIENTO RELLENO DE BACALAO

PEPPERS STUFFED WITH COD

Ingredients: *Red "piquillo" peppers, cod, olive oil, butter, flour, garlic, onion, parsley and egg.*

Method: Make a bechamel sauce with the cod, onion, parsley and garlic. Use this mixture to stuff the peppers, then dip them in flour and egg and fry in hot oil.

CHATKA

CRAB STICKS

Ingredients: *Crab sticks, mayonnaise, boiled prawns and bread.*

Method: Chop the crab sticks and mix with the mayonnaise. Put on a slice of bread and decorate with a peeled boiled prawn.

MEJILLÓN RELLENO

STUFFED MUSSELS

Ingredients: *Mussels, pepper, hard-boiled egg, butter, onion, milk, flour, salt and olive oil.*

Method: Gently fry the onion in the oil and butter. Add the remaining ingredients and make a bechamel sauce. Allow the mixture to cool and then fill the mussel shells with it. Dip in flour, egg and breadcrumbs and fry in plenty of hot oil.

BASQUE
CHAMPI
Bar Basque
COJO-NUDO

B A S Q U E

Miramar nº 5 • Tel.: 943-42 47 47

B A S Q U E

BASQUE

Ingredients: *Bacon, "piquillo" pepper and prawns.*

Method: Make a bacon roll with a peeled prawn and a pepper inside. Spear it on to a cocktail stick so that it doesn't unroll and fry it in plenty of hot oil. Serve hot.

C H A M P I

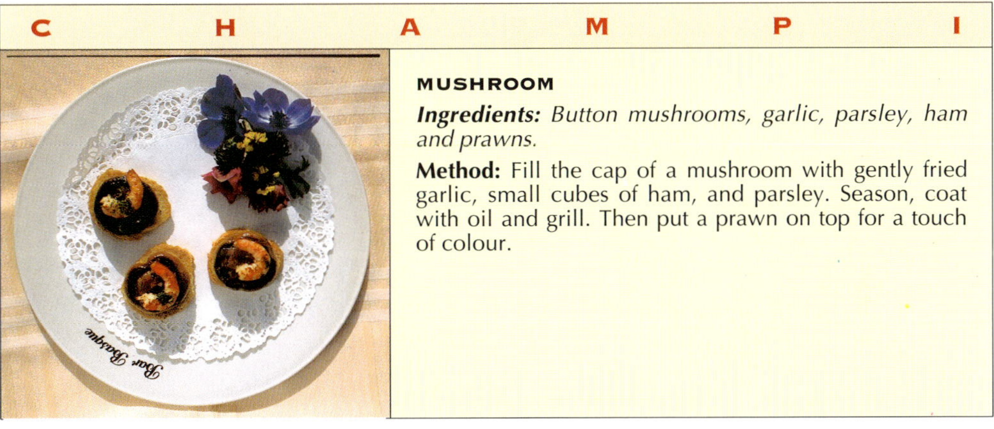

MUSHROOM

Ingredients: *Button mushrooms, garlic, parsley, ham and prawns.*

Method: Fill the cap of a mushroom with gently fried garlic, small cubes of ham, and parsley. Season, coat with oil and grill. Then put a prawn on top for a touch of colour.

C O J O - N U D O

FAN-TASTIC

Ingredients: *Green pepper, bacon, quails' eggs, "piquillo" pepper, "chorizo" sausage and bread.*

Method: Put a gently fried green pepper on to a piece of bread. On top of that add a slice of grilled bacon. On top of that 2 fried quails' eggs and some strips of gently fried "piquillo" pepper. On top of all this put a small piece of "chorizo" sausage.

CHATKA Y ZANAHORIA

ATÚN CON GUINDILLAS

BAVIERA

Larramendi nº 7 • Tel.: 943-21 22 76

TORTILLA DE PATATA CON PIMIENTOS

POTATO OMELETTE WITH PEPPERS

Ingredients: *Potato omelette and "piquillo" peppers.*

Method: Make a normal potato omelette and decorate it with the "piquillo" peppers cut into strips. As well as giving flavour they will make this simple canape look very attractive indeed.

CHATKA Y ZANAHORIA

CRAB STICKS AND CARROT

Ingredients: *Crab sticks, mayonnaise, strips of grated carrot and bread.*

Method: Chop up the crab sticks and mix with the mayonnaise. Put the mixture on to a piece of bread and put the grated carrot on top for decoration.

ATÚN CON GUINDILLAS

TUNA FISH WITH CHILI PEPPERS

Ingredients: *Tuna fish, mayonnaise and chili peppers from Ibarra.*

Method: Flake the tuna fish and mix with the mayonnaise. Put on to a piece of bread and decorate the canape with a pepper not only to enhance its taste, but also its appearance.

TORTILLA DE AJOS TIERNOS

ANCHOA

BAY-BAY

B A Y - B A Y

Avda. Libertad nº 37 • Tel.: 943-42 70 62

T O R T I L L A D E A J O S T I E R N O S

OMELETTE WITH YOUNG GARLIC SHOOTS

Ingredients: *200 g of young garlic shoots, 4 eggs and salt.*

Method: Remove the outer layers and the greenest part of the garlic shoots. Cut them into very small pieces and gently fry in oil in a frying pan. When they are cooked remove them from the pan and mix them in a bowl with the beaten eggs. Make an omelette with this mixture on a low heat so that it does not dry out.

A N C H O A

ANCHOVY

Ingredients: *Sliced bread, smoked anchovy and half a lemon.*

Method: Cut the bread into four pieces and toast. Cut the anchovies in half and arrange on the slice of toast in such a way that the wider part of one half is at one end and the wider part of the other is at the other end of the bread. Add a few drops of lemon juice and always serve with the bread hot.

B A Y - B A Y

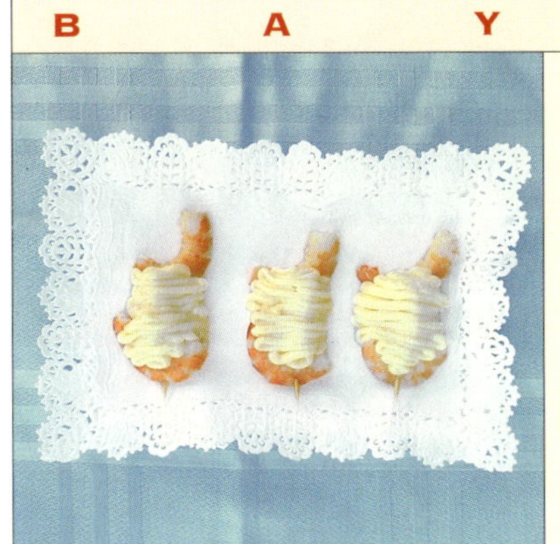

BAY - BAY

Ingredients: *2 large boiled prawns, hard-boiled egg and mayonnaise.*

Method: Spear a quarter of a hard-boiled egg onto a cocktail stick, then put a large peeled prawn at each end and decorate with mayonnaise.

UDABERRI

COCKTAIL BERGARA

DELICIAS DE PATO AL CALVADOS

BERGARA

Gral. Artetxe, C. • Tel.: 943-27 50 26

COCKTAIL BERGARA

BERGARA COCKTAIL

Ingredients: *3 slices of fresh pineapple, 6 large boiled prawn tails, 2 dessertpoonfulls of crab sticks and cocktail sauce.*

Method: Dice the pineapple and prawns. Put them in a bowl together with the chopped crab sticks. Make a cocktail sauce with mayonnaise, tomato ketchup, tabasco sauce and some drops of brandy. Serve on a piece of sliced toasted bread.

UDABERRI

SPRING

Ingredients: *1 medium-sized courgette, half a kilo of peeled Norway lobsters, 50 g of cured ham, 1 glass of cream.*

Method: Gently fry the diced courgette in a little oil for about 10 minutes. Add the cut up Norway lobsters and cream and finally the cured ham cut into cubes. Cook everything for 5 minutes. Serve in pastry cases with chopped parsley.

DELICIAS DE PATO AL CALVADOS

DUCK DELIGHTS WITH CALVADOS

Ingredients: *1 duck breast, 1 apple, 1 clove of garlic, and 1 glass of Calvados*

Method: Fry the duck breast, which has been filleted and has had the fat removed, in 2 dessertspoonfulls of butter. Remove the duck and in the fat that is left gently fry a clove of garlic and a chopped apple. Let it all cook through. Then add the duck and boil everything briefly together with the liqueur. Serve in hot pastry.

TXALUPA

PASTEL DE MARISCO

ANCHOAS EN REVUELTO

ANCHOAS EN REVUELTO

ANCHOVIES IN SCRAMBLED EGG

Ingredients: *100 g of fresh anchovies, "piquillo" peppers, garlic and 1 egg.*

Method: Gently fry the chopped garlic in oil. Add the anchovies and peppers cut into thin julienne strips. Finally add the eggs and cook making sure that they don't get too dry. Serve on toasted bread.

TXALUPA

BOATS

Ingredients: *100 g of button mushrooms, 8 large prawns, 50 g of cured ham, garlic and a glass of cream.*

Method: Fry a clove of garlic together with the chopped mushrooms. Add the peeled prawns and diced ham. Pour in the cream and allow to cook. Pour into pastry cases, sprinkle with grated cheese and grill.

PASTEL DE MARISCO

SEAFOOD COCKTAIL

Ingredients: *6 small Norway prawn tails, 8 large prawns, 2 slices of smoked salmon, 2 "piquillo" peppers, 2 hard-boiled egg yolks, and 1 litre of tomato sauce.*

Method: Crush the egg yolks with the salmon and seafood. Add the peppers and tomato sauce and mix. Serve on fried bread and decorate with grated hard-boiled egg white.

PINCHO DE BACALAO AHUMADO

NIDO DE CODORNIZ

ANCHOA RELLENA DE VERDURITAS

B E T I - J A I

Fermin Calbetón n° 22 • Tel.: 943-42 77 37/42 04 75

PINCHO DE BACALAO AHUMADO

SMOKED COD PINTXO

Ingredients: *Toasted bread, smoked cod, red "piquillo" pepper and olive oil.*

Method: Put the cod and pepper on the bread and sprinkle with a little olive oil.

NIDO DE CODORNIZ

QUAIL'S NEST

Ingredients: *Courgette, pepper, prawn, quail's egg and onion.*

Method: Gently fry the chopped onion and later add the chopped courgette. Let this cook slowly and when everything is soft put into a small pastry case. Decorate with pepper, a prawn, and finally a fried quail's egg.

ANCHOA RELLENA DE VERDURITAS

FRESH ANCHOVY STUFFED WITH VEGETABLES

Ingredients: *Onion, red pepper, green pepper, cleaned fresh anchovies, flour and egg.*

Method: Gently fry the chopped onion and pepper until soft. Stuff the anchovies with this mixture, dip them in flour and egg and fry in very hot oil.

SETAS REBOZADAS

CROISSANT RELLENO

BIDEA

Virgen del Carmen nº 65 • Tel.: 943-27 25 01

SETAS REBOZADAS

MUSHROOMS FRIED IN BATTER

Ingredients: *Button mushrooms, anchovies, green peppers, prawns, oil, garlic, vinegar and bread.*

Method: Fry the mushrooms in the oil together with the finely chopped garlic and add some vinegar.Allow to stand for a while. Then coat the mushrooms in flour and egg and fry. Put on a piece of bread and decorate with a green pepper, an anchovy and a boiled, peeled prawn.

CROISSANT RELLENO

STUFFED CROISSANT

Ingredients: *Croissant, lettuce, crab stick, boiled prawns, egg and mayonnaise.*

Method: Cut a small croissant in half. Fill with chopped lettuce, crab stick, prawns, boiled egg and mayonnaise. Garnish by holding it open with a prawn.

FUNDIDO

MELTED CHEESE

Ingredients: *Cured ham, boiled ham, cheese, mayonnaise, prawn, hard-boiled egg and bread.*

Method: Melt the cheese and put it on a piece of bread with the boiled ham and cured ham. Decorate with mayonnaise, chopped ham, cheese and a boiled prawn.

MORROS

ANCHOA EN COMPAÑÍA

ENSALADA
DE SALMÓN

BODEGA DONOSTIARRA

Matía nº 36 • Tel.: 943-2115 59

M O R R O S

MUZZLES

Ingredients: *Muzzles, chef's choice of vegetables for boiling the muzzles, tomato, chili peppers, bacon fat and "chorizo" sausage. For the sauce: chopped onion, garlic and green pepper.*

Method: Boil the cleaned muzzles with the vegetables. While they are cooking make a sauce by cooking all the ingredients gently and thoroughly in oil. When this is ready add the "chorizo" sausage, the bacon fat, the chili pepper and fry everything together. Finally add the muzzles and allow them to cook for 5 minutes. Serve on a plate.

A N C H O A E N C O M P A Ñ Í A

ANCHOVIES IN COMPANY

Ingredients: *Anchovy, salmon, large prawns and vinaigrette with peppers.*

Method: Put the anchovies on the bread and cover with vinaigrette. Put a slice of smoked salmon and a large boiled large prawn on top and cover everything with vinagrette once again.

E N S A L A D A D E S A L M Ó N

SALMON SALAD

Ingredients: *Salmon, large prawns, lettuce and mayonnaise.*

Method: Chop up all the ingredients and mix them with the mayonnaise. Spread on pieces of bread.

CHATKA

PIMIENTOS
RELLENOS
DE BACALAO

PUDÍN DE
MERLUZA
Y GAMBAS

BUZTINTXULO

Buztintxulo nº 14 • Tel.: 943-27 83 96

PIMIENTOS RELLENOS DE BACALAO

PEPPERS STUFFED WITH COD

Ingredients: *"Piquillo" peppers, salt cod, flour, milk, cream, onion and butter.*

Method: Gently fry the finely chopped onion and when it has browned add the cod. When it is cooked mix with a light bechamel sauce and stuff the peppers with this mixture. To make the sauce blend "piquillo" pepper and cream and pour over the stuffed peppers.

CHATKA

CRAB STICKS

Ingredients: *Crab sticks, mayonnaise, egg and bread.*

Method: Chop the crab sticks and mix with the mayonnaise. Put on to a piece of bread and garnish with grated hard-boiled egg.

PUDÍN DE MERLUZA Y GAMBAS

HAKE AND PRAWN PUDDING

Ingredients: *7 eggs, 250 cc of cream, 250 cc of tomato, hake, and prawns.*

Method: Boil the hake and prawns and put them to one side. Beat the eggs, cream and tomato and add the prawns and fish to it. Pour this mixture into a pudding mould which has been lined with butter and breadcrumbs. Cook in a hot oven bain marie until it sets.

CRÊPES IRATI

PIMIENTOS DEL
PIQUILLO
DONOSTIARRAS

PASTEL UDABERRI

CAFETERÍA LOREA

Tolosa nº 111 • Tel.: 943-21 33 98

CRÊPES IRATI

IRATI PANCAKES

Ingredients: *Large prawns, button mushrooms, garlic, white wine, corn flour and salt.*

Method: Make the pancake batter by beating an egg with flour, milk and salt. Make the pancakes with a little butter. Then gently fry the large prawns, mushrooms and garlic. When they are done, put some of this mixture onto each of the pancakes and roll them up. Serve hot.

PIMIENTOS DEL PIQUILLO DONOSTIARRAS

"PIQUILLO" PEPPERS SAN SEBASTIAN STYLE

Ingredients: *"Piquillo" peppers, fresh squid, sachets of squid ink, onion, parsley, garlic and flour.*

Method: Fry the squid with the onion and garlic. Prepare the squid ink with very finely chopped onion. Stuff the peppers with the squid and serve on a dish with the ink sauce underneath. Sprinkle with finely chopped parsley.

PASTEL UDABERRI

SPRING TART

Ingredients: *Red pepper, spinach, crab sticks, hake, mayonnaise, caviar, cream, tomato, egg, salt, pepper, tomato and sliced bread.*

Method: Prepare three different puddings separately. One with red pepper, one with spinach and crab stick, and one with hake. When they are ready cut a circular piece out of each one and put on the toasted bread. Finally garnish with a little mayonnaise and caviar.

TARTALETA USOA

BROCHETA LOREA

COCKTAIL CANTÁBRIC

TARTALETA USOA

USOA TARTLETS

Ingredients: *Calves' brains, spinach, salt, garlic, "piquillo peppers" and egg.*

Method: Boil the calves' brains and spinach separately. Cut the peppers into fine strips and fry with the finely chopped garlic. Then make this into a scrambled egg dish with the brains and spinach. Season the mixture and use it to fill the tartlets. Garnish with some strips of pepper.

BROCHETA LOREA

LOREA KEBABS

Ingredients: *Button mushrooms, prawns, Gernika green peppers, hot red peppers, "piquillo" peppers, salt, garlic, parsley, oil and vinegar.*

Method: Put all the ingredients on to kebab skewers and grill. Season to taste. If desired, serve with a garlic sauce poured over the grilled kebab.

COCKTAIL CANTÁBRICO

BAY OF BISCAY COCKTAIL

Ingredients: *Small crab, prawns, mussels, crab sticks, caviar, lettuce cut into thin (julienne) strips, mayonnaise and tomato ketchup.*

Method: Boil the small crabs, prawns, mussels and crab sticks. Cut the lettuce into thin julienne strips and prepare a cocktail sauce with mayonnaise and ketchup. Put a base of letttuce into some tartlets and add a little cocktail sauce. Chop all the shellfish and mix in a bowl. Then put some of it into each of the tarlets and garnish with the caviar.

CAPRICIS

TARTALETAS

MARI JOSE

CAPRICIS

Carlos I nº 2 • Tel.: 943-46 58 56

CAPRICIS

CAPRICIS

Ingredients: *Toasted bread, crab sticks, smoked salmon, pippin apple, milk mayonnaise.*

Method: Boil the apple and mix with the flaked crab sticks. Add the mayonnaise and mix thoroughly. Then put the mixture on to the bread. Decorate with a piece of smoked salmon on top.

TARTALETAS

TARTLETS

Ingredients: *Small pastry cases, prawn tails, whisky, milk, oil, salt, vinegar and fresh tomato sauce.*

Method: Mix all the ingredients apart from the pastry cases and prawns. When you have a thick creamy filling, put some into each tartlet. Decorate with a prawn tail on top.

MARI JOSE

MARI JOSE

Ingredients: *Sliced bread, crab sticks, lettuce, boiled ham and milk mayonnaise.*

Method: Chop the crab sticks, lettuce and ham and mix with the mayonnaise. Spread on to a slice of bread and then cut into quarters to make 4 canapes.

PIMIENTOS RELLENOS

AMARA

TITO

PIMIENTOS RELLENOS

STUFFED PEPPERS

Ingredients: *"Piquillo" peppers, garlic, parsley, tuna fish in oil, hard-boiled egg yolk, prawns.*

Method: Make a filling with the egg yolk, tuna fish and prawns. Use it to stuff the peppers, which have previously been warmed with the garlic. Decorate with chopped garlic and parsley. Serve on a slice of toasted bread.

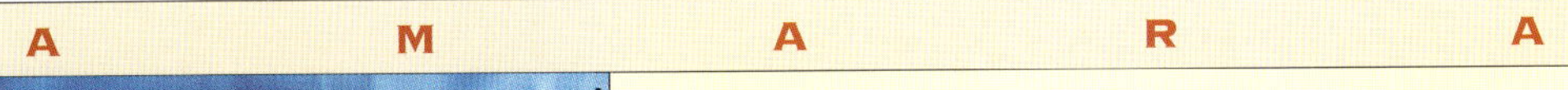

AMARA

AMARA

Ingredients: *Sliced bread, hard-boiled egg white, smoked salmon, chopped spring onion, tuna fish in oil, and milk mayonnaise.*

Method: Mix the chopped salmon, the hard-boiled egg yolk, the chopped spring onion and the tuna fish. Mix with the mayonnaise and spread on to a piece of toasted sliced bread. Cut into 4 squares and garnish with a piece of salmon and the hard-boiled egg white.

TITO

TITO

Ingredients: *Sliced bread, large boiled prawn tails, fresh tomato, tuna fish in oil, red pepper, hard-boiled egg and milk mayonnaise.*

Method: Cut the bread into squares and on each piece put a very thin slice of tomato, some flaked tuna fish mixed with mayonnaise, a pepper cut into thin strips and the hard-boiled egg. Cover with mayonnaise and grated hard-boiled egg white. Decorate with large prawn tail.

TXALOTA DE BACALAO
Y CALABACÍN

PINTXO DE TOMATE Y
RAPE CARMENCITA

CASCANUECES

Paseo Colon nº 46 • Tel: 943-290124

TXALOTA DE BACALAO Y CALABACÍN

COD WITH SPRING ONION AND COURGETTE

Ingredients: *200 g of flaked de-salted cod, 2 courgettes, 1 green pepper, 1 red pepper, 1 onion, 3 cloves of garlic, 2 ripe tomatoes, olive oil.*

Method: In the olive oil gently fry a chopped clove of garlic, a chopped onion, a courgette and a diced tomato. Season and add the cod. Put this mixture to one side. Cut the other courgette into thin slices, dip in flour and fry in oil until it has just browned. Use the courgette to line a round, pudding-type mould. Put the cod mixture in the centre. Cover with more slices of courgette, press down and keep in the fridge for 24 hours.

ANCHOAS MARINADAS SOBRE PIMIENTO

MARINADED ANCHOVIES ON PEPPERS

Ingredients: *12 anchovies, salt, a glass of Sherry vinegar, olive oil, garlic, chopped parsley and 3 peppers.*

Method: Season the anchovies and marinade in vinegar for 6 hours. After that clean them and put them in oil with garlic and parsley. Cut the pepper into thick strips and gently poach in oil with garlic.

PINTXO DE TOMATE Y RAPE CARMENCITA

CARMENCITA'S TOMATO AND MONKFISH PINTXO

Ingredients: *4 slices of ripe tomato, half a kg of monkfish, 2 eggs, salt, oil, garlic and parsley.*

Method: Season the tomato slices, dip them in flour and egg and fry. Cut the monkfish into thin slices, season and soak in a mixture of egg, parsley and garlic for about half an hour. Grill first on one side, then on the other.

PATATAS AL AJILLO

MIXTO

PASTA DE GAMBAS

C I A B O G A

Easo nº 9 • Tel: 943-422926

P A T A T A S   A L   A J I L L O

GARLIC POTATOES

Ingredients: *Garlic, parsley, potatoes and oil.*

Method: Cut the potato into small pieces and parboil. Fry in a deep-fryer. When they are fried, put them in an earthenware dish and add very finely chopped and gently fried garlic and parsley.

M I X T O

MELANGE

Ingredients: *Cheese, cured ham, anchovies in oil, hard-boiled egg and bread.*

Method: Cut the cheese and put it on the bread. Put a slice of cured ham on top. On top of that put the chopped egg and garnish with an anchovy.

P A S T A   D E   G A M B A S

PRAWN PATE

Ingredients: *Tuna fish, prawns, hard-boiled egg and bread.*

Method: Mince a little tuna fish, a few boiled prawns and a hard-boiled egg to form a paste. Spread this on a piece of bread and garnish with a boiled prawn and grated hard-boiled egg.

SALPICÓN DE HONGOS
Y ENSALADA

TOSTA DE MORRO

CHIPIRÓN TROCEADO EN SU TINTA

CLERY

31 de Agosto nº 7 • Tel: 943-42 34 01

SALPICÓN DE HONGOS Y ENSALADA

EDIBLE FUNGI AND SALAD COCKTAIL

Ingredients: *Sautéd edible fungi, smoked salmon, mayonnaise, lettuce, curly endive, imitation caviar, bread and salt.*

Method: Chop the fungi and salmon; cut the lettuce and endive into thin (julienne) strips and mix everything with the mayonnaise. Cut the bread into slices, spread the cocktail on top and garnish with a dot of mayonnaise and some caviar.

TOSTA DE MORROS

MUZZLES ON TOAST

Ingredients: *Muzzles, garlic, oil, onion, thyme, white wine, stock, leek, salt and bread.*

Method: Wash the muzzles thoroughly, Put a little oil plus the finely chopped onion, garlic and leek into a pressure cooker. Add a little thyme, salt and wine. Then put in the muzzles with just enough stock to moisten everything. Cook for an hour and a half. When the muzzles are cooked, strain the liquid. Cut the muzzles into thin slices, arrange them on top of slices of fried bread and pour a little sauce over them.

CHIPIRÓN TROCEADO EN SU TINTA

CHOPPED SQUID IN INK

Ingredients: *Large squid, garlic, onion, green pepper, tomato, oil, white wine, "fumet" (concentrated fish stock), rice, salt and parsley.*

Method: Clean the squid thoroughly and cut into thin strips. Toss in a little oil and garlic until they brown. For the sauce gently fry garlic, onion, chopped green pepper in oil in a saucepan. Add a little tomato, white wine and "fumet" and allow to cook. When it is cooked blend it and then strain it. Add the sachets of squid ink. Season, mix the squid with the sauce and allow to boil for about 10 minutes.

PINTXO CHOMIN

TRES COLORES

ZABALETA

C H O M I N

Zabaleta nº 17 • Tel: 943-27 92 16

P I N T X O   C H O M I N

CHOMIN PINTXO

Ingredients: *Bread, smoked salmon, hard-boiled egg, prawns, anchovies in oil.*

Method: Put the salmon on to a slice of bread. Then cut the egg and put a slice on top of the salmon, followed by a prawn and an anchovy fillet to finish. Finally pour a little oil over the anchovies.

T R E S   C O L O R E S

THREE COLOURS

Ingredients: *Bread, cured ham, green pepper, "morron" red pepper, anchovies in oil.*

Method: Fry the green pepper and put a strip of it on to a slice of bread. Then put a piece of cured ham, and another strip of green pepper on top. Then add two strips of red pepper on either side of the green and lastly the anchovy.

Z A B A L E T A

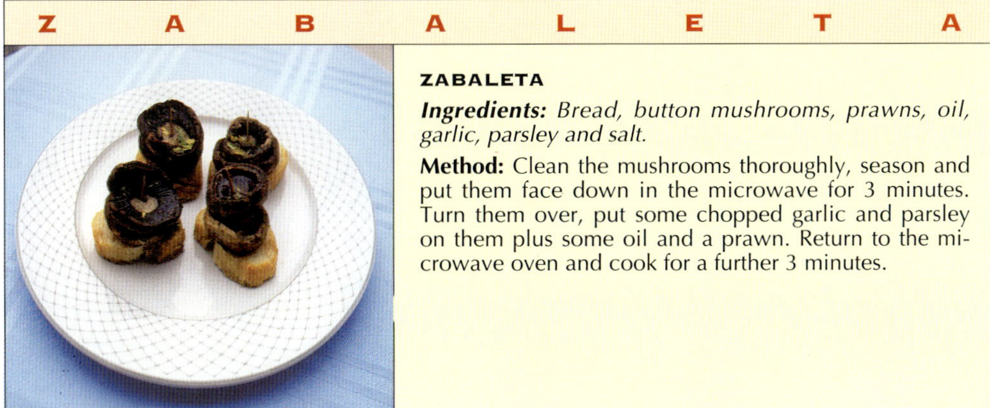

ZABALETA

Ingredients: *Bread, button mushrooms, prawns, oil, garlic, parsley and salt.*

Method: Clean the mushrooms thoroughly, season and put them face down in the microwave for 3 minutes. Turn them over, put some chopped garlic and parsley on them plus some oil and a prawn. Return to the microwave oven and cook for a further 3 minutes.

SALMÓN CON JAMÓN Y MAHONESA

HUEVITOS [illegible]
CODORNIZ
CON JAMÓN

DAKAR

DAKAR

Eustasio Amilibia nº 9 • Tel: 943-46 21 43

SALMÓN CON JAMÓN Y MAHONESA

SALMON WITH BOILED HAM AND MAYONNAISE

Ingredients: *Smoked salmon, boiled ham and mayonnaise.*

Method: Chop up the salmon and the ham. Mix with the mayonnaise and spread on to a piece of bread.

HUEVITO DE CODORNIZ CON JAMÓN

QUAIL'S EGG WITH HAM

Ingredients: *Quail's egg, cured ham, "chorizo" chipolata and green pepper.*

Method: Put a slice of ham on to a piece of bread. Then the fried chipolata and fried egg. Garnish with a strip of fried green pepper.

DAKAR

DAKAR

Ingredients: *Fresh anchovies, blue cheese, salt, flour, egg, oil and butter*

Method: When you have cleaned the anchovies put two together as if they were a sandwich and between them put a cream made of blue cheese and butter. Dip the anchovies in flour and egg and fry gently in plenty of oil.

SALMÓN RELLENO
MOUSSE DE OCA
CON CHAMPIS
CODORNI

D A N E N A

Matía nº 6 • Tel: 943-21 73 21

SALMÓN RELLENO

STUFFED SALMON

Ingredients: *Smoked salmon, onion, tuna fish, crab sticks, mayonnaise.*

Method: To make the stuffing finely chop the onion, add the flaked tuna fish and chopped crab sticks. Add plenty of mayonnaise. Spread out a slice of smoked salmon, fill with the stuffing and make into a roll. Garnish to taste.

MOUSSE DE OCA CON CHAMPIS

GOOSE MOUSSE WITH BUTTON MUSHROOMS

Ingredients: *Goose mousse, thinly sliced button mushrooms, parsley, oil, garlic, pepper and sweet sherry.*

Method: Put a little oil in a frying plan and add finely chopped garlic and parsley and then the mushrooms. Toss in the oil, add a little sweet sherry and season. Put a slice of goose mousse onto a piece of toasted bread and cover it with the slices of mushroom. Garnish with some thin strips of goose fat.

CODORNIZ

QUAILS

Ingredients: *Quails, sherry vinegar, brandy, pepper, thyme, oil, butter, salt and beans.*

Method: Cut the quail open in half lengthwise. Pour on a little vinegar, brandy and sprinkle on some white pepper and thyme. Allow to marinade for 30 minutes. Put a little butter and oil in a frying pan. When hot, fry the quail with the skin downwards. When the meat changes colour, turn it over and fry a little more. Pour a glass of brandy into the fat that remains in the frying pan. Heat and flambé it. Garnish with the beans.

CHAMPI RELLENO Y REBOZADO

ANCHOA RELLENA

TXITXARRO

CHAMPI RELLENO Y REBOZADO

STUFFED MUSHROOMS IN BATTER

Ingredients: *Button mushrooms, salt, oil, white pepper, garlic, chopped cured ham and a thick bechamel sauce.*

Method: Clean the mushrooms and remove the stalks. Put a little salt, pepper, a few drops of oil, a little chopped garlic, a little cured ham and a tablespoonful of white sauce into the cap of one of the mushrooms. Put another mushroom cap on top and press down a little. Dip in flour, egg and breadcrumbs and fry in plenty of hot oil. Garnish with a little white sauce.

ANCHOA RELLENA

STUFFED ANCHOVY

Ingredients: *Anchovies, fried green pepper, processed cheese, chopped garlic and pepper.*

Method: Clean and open the anchovies. Take an open anchovy and put a little salt, a strip of green pepper, a little chopped garlic, a little pepper and a strip of cheese. Cover with another anchovy. Dip in flour and egg and fry in hot oil. Garnish to taste.

TXITXARRO

HORSE MACKEREL

Ingredients: *Horse mackerel, potatoes, garlic, red and green pepper, oil, vinegar, salt and onion.*

Method: Peel the potatoes and cut them into slices half a centimetre thick. Remove the scales from the fish and fillet it. Cut the green pepper and onion into thin (julienne) strips and fry them. Put a little oil in a frying pan and toss the mackerel fillets in it. Take a slice of potato and put a fillet of mackerel on top. Brown some sliced garlic in oil in a frying pan. Add a little vinegar. Put some strips of fried pepper and onion on top of the mackerel and potato and cover with the fried garlic, oil and vinegar mixture.

DESY
RONDA
GROS

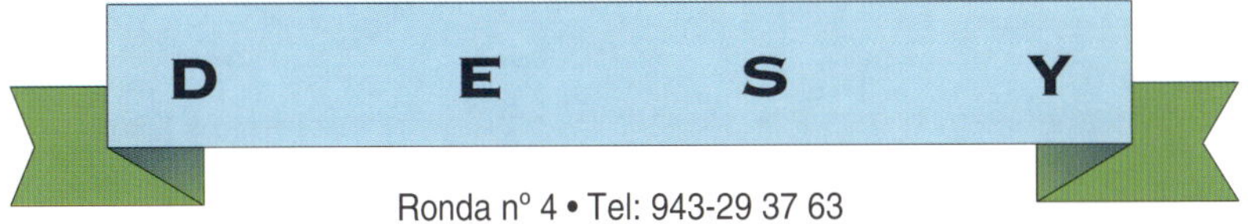

DESY

Ronda nº 4 • Tel: 943-29 37 63

D E S Y

DESY

Ingredients: *Green pepper, anchovies in oil, vinaigrette, red pepper, large prawn and toasted bread.*

Method: Put a green pepper on top of the toasted bread. Put an anchovy and a large prawn on top of the green pepper and cover with vinaigrette. At the other end put a little chopped "morron"red pepper.

R O N D A

RONDA

Ingredients: *Wholemeal bread, boiled ham, mayonnaise and a large boiled prawn.*

Method: Chop the ham and mix it with the mayonnaise. Put some of this mixture on top of a piece of wholemeal bread and garnish with a prawn cut in half.

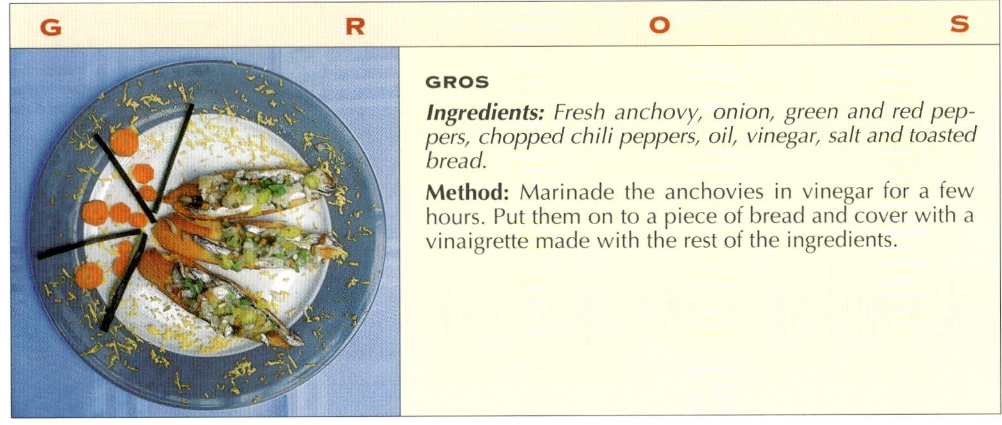

G R O S

GROS

Ingredients: *Fresh anchovy, onion, green and red peppers, chopped chili peppers, oil, vinegar, salt and toasted bread.*

Method: Marinade the anchovies in vinegar for a few hours. Put them on to a piece of bread and cover with a vinaigrette made with the rest of the ingredients.

SALMÓN
BROCHETA
TARTALETA

S A L M Ó N

SALMON

Ingredients: *Sliced bread, cocktail sauce, hard-boiled egg white and large chopped prawns and smoked salmon.*

Method: Mix the cocktail sauce with the hard-boiled egg white and large prawns. Spread this mixture on to the bread and garnish with some strips of smoked salmon.

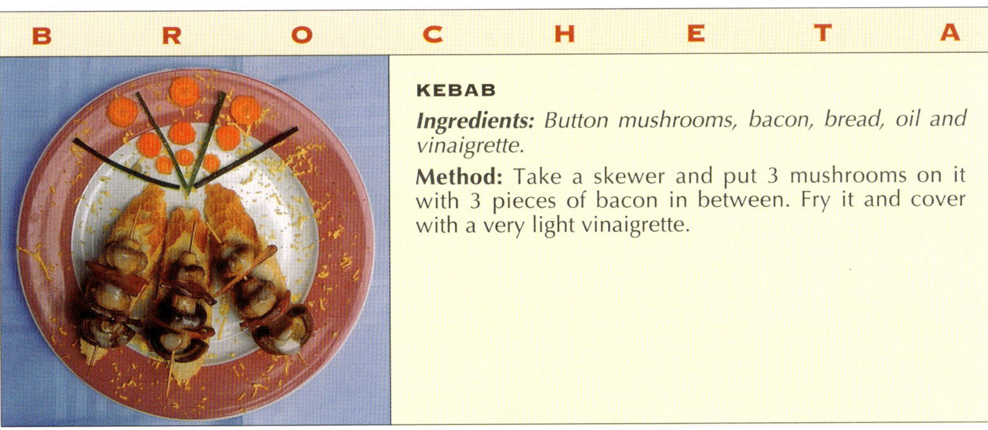

B R O C H E T A

KEBAB

Ingredients: *Button mushrooms, bacon, bread, oil and vinaigrette.*

Method: Take a skewer and put 3 mushrooms on it with 3 pieces of bacon in between. Fry it and cover with a very light vinaigrette.

T A R T A L E T A

TARTLETS

Ingredients: *Pastry cases, boiled chicken, lettuce, sweet corn and mayonnaise.*

Method: Make a filling with the chopped chicken, the finely chopped lettuce, the sweet corn and the mayonnaise. Fill the pastry cases with it and put a garnish of sweet corn on top.

TORTILLA RELLENA

REVUELTO DE AJOS
TIERNOS Y GAMBAS

DONIBANE

Zabaleta nº 26 • Tel.:943-29 09 85

TORTILLA RELLENA

STUFFED OMELETTE

Ingredients: *Eggs, potatoes, onion, crab sticks, lettuce and mayonnaise.*

Method: Make an omelette with the eggs, potatoes and onion and allow to cool. When it is cold slice it in half horizontally. Spread plenty of mayonnaise on to one half and cover with a layer of lettuce and then a layer of flaked crab sticks. Then cover this with the other half of the omelette and serve on a piece of toasted sliced bread.

ENSALADA PRIMAVERA

SPRING SALAD

Ingredients: *Boiled ham, lettuce, red pepper, tomato, prawns, mayonnaise, egg.*

Method: Finely dice all the ingredients but put a prawn to one side. Add the mayonnaise and spread the mixture onto a piece of bread. Lastly cover with some grated egg white and a prawn.

REVUELTO DE AJOS TIERNOS Y GAMBAS

SCRAMBLED EGG WITH YOUNG GARLIC SHOOTS AND PRAWNS

Ingredients: *3 cloves of garlic, young garlic shoots, prawns and eggs.*

Method: In a frying pan toss the finely chopped garlic cloves, the young garlic shoots, and the prawns. Season and add the lightly beaten eggs. Spread on to crispbread taking care not to let the crispbread get too soggy. Garnish with chopped parsley.

EGAÑA

AURORA

CRISTINA

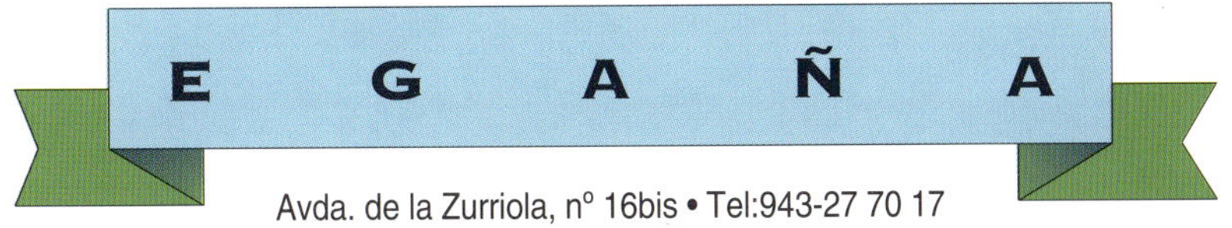

E G A Ñ A

Avda. de la Zurriola, nº 16bis • Tel:943-27 70 17

E G A Ñ A

EGAÑA

Ingredients: *Green chili peppers, anchovies, fried bread, and "piquillo" peppers.*

Method: Chop the peppers, the chili peppers and anchovies very finely. Mix them together. Fry the bread and spread the mixture on to the slices.

A U R O R A

AURORA

Ingredients: *Olives, green chili peppers, tuna fish and asparagus. Vinaigrette made with onion and parsley.*

Method: Spear all the ingredients on to a cocktail stick. Cover with the vinaigrette.

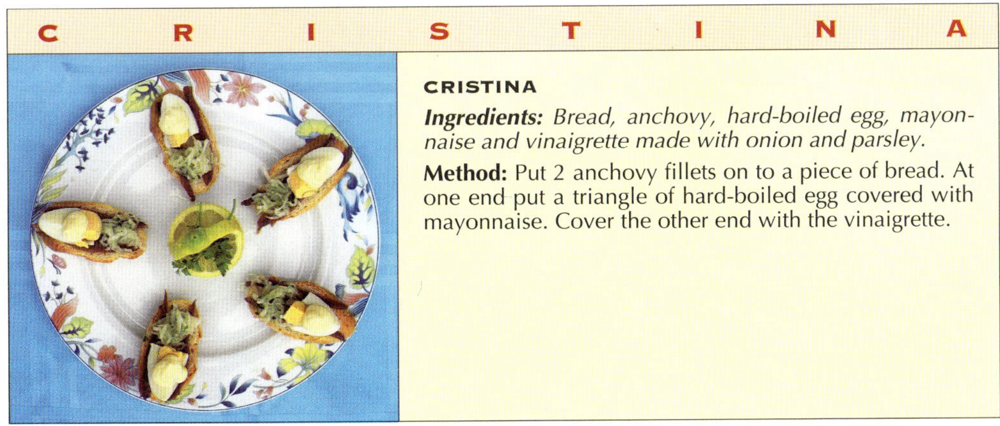

C R I S T I N A

CRISTINA

Ingredients: *Bread, anchovy, hard-boiled egg, mayonnaise and vinaigrette made with onion and parsley.*

Method: Put 2 anchovy fillets on to a piece of bread. At one end put a triangle of hard-boiled egg covered with mayonnaise. Cover the other end with the vinaigrette.

BROCHETA DE LANGOSTINOS

BACALAO ENCEBOLLADO

PINTXO EGOSARI

EGOSARI

Fermin Calbetón, nº15 • Tel:943-42 82 10/42 57 80

BROCHETA DE LANGOSTINOS

LARGE PRAWN KEBAB

Ingredients: *4 squares of bacon, 4 large prawns and 4 mushrooms.*

Method: Take a 25cm long skewer and spear the pieces of mushroom, bacon and large prawn on to it alternately. Grill the kebab until the prawns have browned. Serve with a tablespoonful of vinaigrette poured over it.

BACALAO ENCEBOLLADO

COD COOKED IN ONION

Ingredients: *Fried cod, green peppers, onion and olive oil.*

Method: Cut the fillets of cod into pieces of about 50g each and remove the bones. Dip the pieces in flour and fry in olive oil with some sliced garlic. In another pan gently fry the green peppers and onion cut into thin (julienne) strips. Put the pieces of cod onto slices of bread and cover with the fried peppers and onion.

PINTXO EGOSARI

EGOSARI PINTXO

Ingredients: *Toasted bread, a small green Gernika pepper, anchovy in oil, onion, pepper, large prawns and strips of red pepper.*

Method: Put a Gernika green pepper on to a piece of toasted bread, followed by two anchovies. Then add the onion and the red pepper, which have been cut into strips and gently fried. Put a large prawn on top of all this and garnish with some strips of red pepper.

BROCHETA DE ALCACHOFAS

HOGAZA DE LOMO

PINTXO PENI

EL ÁLAMO

Duque de Mandas nº 19 • Tel:943-28 66 19

BROCHETA DE ALCACHOFAS

ARTICHOKE KEBAB

Ingredients: *Artichokes, onion, eggs, "piquillo" peppers, asparagus, anchovies and vinaigrette dressing.*

Method: Prepare the kebabs with pieces of artichoke alternating with pieces of asparagus. Put a piece of hard-boiled egg at one end. Garnish with an anchovy in oil and cover with the vinaigrette.

HOGAZA DE LOMO

PORK CHINE LOAF

Ingredients: *Sliced bread, processed cheese, marinaded loin of pork, and "piquillo" peppers.*

Method: Toast a slice a bread and put a slice of cheese on top. Cook the pork and peppers separately and when the pork is cooked put it onto the cheese together with the peppers.

PINTXO PENI

PENI CANAPE

Ingredients: *Homemade bread, cream cheese, walnuts and dates.*

Method: Toast the bread and when it has cooled spread some cheese on to it. Put a shelled walnut and a date cut in half on top.

BOLSITA DE TXANGURRO

ENSALADILLA
“EL FARO”

ROLLITO DE
PIMIENTO VERDE
Y GAMBAS

EL FARO

Secundino Esnaola nº 46 • Tel: 943-32 17 47

BOLSITA DE TXANGURRO

SPIDER CRAB POUCHES

Ingredients: *Savoury pancakes, onion, flaked spider crab, leek, bay leaf, olive oil and a dash of brandy.*

Method: Chop the onion, leek and a little piece of bay leaf. Gently fry them in olive oil and when they are done, add the spider crab and the brandy. Bring everything to the boil and then fill the pancakes with the mixture to make little pouches.

ENSALADILLA "EL FARO"

"EL FARO" SALAD

Ingredients: *Boiled ham, curly endive, lettuce heart, hard-boiled egg, mayonnaise or cocktail sauce.*

Method: Dice all the ingredients. Add the mayonnaise or cocktail sauce and mix thoroughly. Spread onto pieces of toasted bread.

ROLLITO DE PIMIENTO VERDE Y GAMBAS

GREEN PEPPER AND PRAWN ROLLS

Ingredients: *Green pepper, peeled prawns, onion, olive oil, cream of shellfish, bechamel sauce, a square of savoury sponge cake, salt and white pepper.*

Method: Gently fry the onion and green pepper (not too finely chopped). When they are done add the pawns and cream of shellfish plus a little white sauce to bind everything together. Season. Take the square of sponge cake and spread the mixture on top. Make it into a roll and cut into slices.

CAPELLO RELLENO DE RABO DE BUEY Y SETAS

CRUJIENTES DE TXITXARROS CON PIMIENTOS VERDES

BARQUETA D PIMIENTOS ASADOS Y ANCHOAS EN VINAGRE

EL NAVARRO

San Martin nº 38 • Tel: 943-42 40 22

CAPELLO RELLENO DE RABO DE BUEY Y SETAS

CABBAGE STUFFED WITH OXTAIL AND MUSHROOMS

Ingredients: *1 cabbage, 1 kg of oxtail, 250 g of mushrooms, 3 onions, 2 carrots, 2 leeks, 1 ripe tomato, 2 cloves of garlic, a glass of oil, red wine, a glass of brandy, salt and white pepper.*

Method: Season the oxtail, fry in the oil and add the vegetables, brandy and red wine. Reduce the sauce and cover with consomé or water. Cook until the oxtail has softened. Then separate the meat from the bones. Gently fry a little onion and add the mushrooms. When they are done add the oxtail meat. Blend the sauce and add some to the onion, mushrooms and oxtail. Boil for about 3 minutes.

CRUJIENTES DE TXITXARRO CON PIMIENTOS VERDES

CRISPY HORSE MACKEREL WITH GREEN PEPPERS

Ingredients: *I horse mackerel, a glass of oil, chopped garlic, salt, parsley and 3 green peppers. For the "Orly" batter: 1 teaspoonful of yeast, 2 eggs, a glass of beer, salt, 1 litre of milk and half a kilo of flour.*

Method: Fillet the fish and cut into sticks about 5 cm long and 1cm wide. Soak for two hours in the oil, chopped garlic, salt and parsley. Prepare the "Orly" batter. Fry the green peppers, peel and cut into strips. Dip the fish in the batter, fry in hot fat and twist the strips of green pepper around the pieces of fish.

BARQUETA DE PIMIENTOS ASADOS Y ANCHOAS EN VINAGRE

BAKED PEPPERS AND ANCHOVIES IN VINEGAR ON FRIED BREAD

Ingredients: *1 kg of anchovies, wine vinegar, some light olive oil(maximum acidity 0.4°), chopped garlic, parsley, salt and 1 kg of red peppers.*

Method: Clean the anchovies and remove the backbone. Allow to marinade in vinegar for 8 hours. Drain thoroughly and season. Add chopped garlic, parsley and oil. Bake the peppers and remove the skins. Cut a slice of bread and fry it in hot oil. Put some baked pepper and then some anchovies on top.

MORCILLA COCIDA
CON BERZA

KOKOTXAS EN
SALSA VERDE

BACALAO CON
PIMIENTO ROJO
Y VERDE

E L U R R A

Gral. Echagüe, nº 7-9 • Tel: 943-42 03 57

MORCILLA COCIDA CON BERZA

BOILED BLACK PUDDING WITH CABBAGE

Ingredients: *Half a kilo of black pudding made with onion and bacon fat, a finely chopped cabbage, olive oil and salt.*

Method: Boil the cabbage for 20 minutes and add oil and salt. When it is cooked put to one side. In another saucepan gently boil the black pudding with a tablespoonful of salt for 20 minutes. Keep covered. When the black pudding has cooked, cut it up and add the cabbage.

KOKOTXAS EN SALSA VERDE

HAKE "KOKOTXAS" IN PARSLEY SAUCE

Ingredients: *1 kilo of hake "kokotxas"(throats of the hake), 1 head of garlic, 1 tablespoonful of salt, 3 or 4 hot chili peppers, and 2 tablespoonfulls of finely chopped parsley.*

Method: Pour a little oil into an earthenware dish. When it is hot, add finely chopped garlic and brown. Put in the "kokotxas". Allow to cook for 30 minutes. Then add the chili peppers and cook gently for a further 5 minutes. Finally sprinkle with parsley and remove from the heat.

BACALAO CON PIMIENTO ROJO Y VERDE

SALT COD WITH RED AND GREEN PEPPERS

Ingredients: *2 kg of cod cut into pieces, a quarter of a litre of olive oil, a quarter of a kilo of fresh green pepper, a quarter of a kilo of fresh red pepper, 2 heads of garlic and a quarter of a litre of soya oil.*

Method: Warm the olive oil in a pan. Add 1 chopped head of garlic and gently cook for a few minutes. Put in the cod and cook gently for 20-30 minutes covered. In another pan gently fry the other head of garlic cut into slices in the soya oil. Add the peppers cut into strips and stir occasionally. Allow to cook for 15 minutes. When they are cooked add the desired amount of cod.

ROLLOS DE PIMIENTO VERDE

HUEVITO

BROCHETA

ENPARANTZA

Plaza del Chofre, nº14 • Tel.:943-29 30 46

ROLLOS DE PIMIENTO VERDE

GREEN PEPPER ROLLS

Ingredients: *Green pepper, boiled ham, cheese.*

Method: Fry the peppers on a very low heat taking care they do not brown. Roll a slice of ham with cheese and cover with the green pepper and roll again to keep the shape. Serve on toasted bread. They can be eaten cold or slighty warmed up.

HUEVITO

LITTLE EGGS

Ingredients: *Hard-boiled egg, cured ham, anchovies and large prawns.*

Method: Cut the hard-boiled egg in half. On top put the anchovy and large peeled prawn. Spear everything on to a cocktail stick. Serve on fried bread with butter and a slice of cured ham on one side. Grate a little egg on top.

BROCHETA

KEBABS

Ingredients: *Bacon, large prawns.*

Method: Take 2 large prawns. Peel them. Roll them in a slice of bacon and spear on to a cocktail stick. Either grill throroughly or crisp them up in the micowave oven. This is a very easy, tasty pintxo.

ALCACHOFITAS

ENPARANTZA

HUEVO Y
JAMÓN YORK

A L C A C H O F I T A S

SMALL ARTICHOKES

Ingredients: *Artichoke hearts, crab sticks, large prawns, olives, salmon, vinaigrette (onion, red and green pepper, salt, oil and wine vinegar).*

Method: Put an artichoke, half a crab stick, a large prawn and an olive on to a cocktail stick and place a strip of smoked salmon on top with each end attached to the two ends of the cocktail stick. Dress with the vinaigrette made with one part of oil to two of vinegar, a pinch of salt, and finely chopped onion.

E N P A R A N T Z A

EMPARANTZA

Ingredients: *Red cabbage, crab stick, large prawn, small prawn, lettuce hearts from Tudela, mayonnaise and tabasco sauce.*

Method: Finely chop all the ingredients and mix with the mayonnaise. Add some drops of tabasco sauce and decorate with a large prawn. This very tasty, attractive canapé is served on a slice of toasted bread.

H U E V O Y J A M Ó N Y O R K

BOILED HAM AND EGG

Ingredients: *Boiled ham, hard-boiled egg, mayonnaise and large prawns.*

Method: Prepare a spread by finely chopping the ham and egg and binding them together with the mayonnaise. Put two slices of hard-boiled egg on to a slice of toasted bread and some of the spread on top. Grate a little hard-boiled egg yolk on top and finally add two large prawns.

BARQUETA DE BONITO

ERDIKO

SALMÓN

ERDIKO

Autonomía nº 1 • Tel.: 943-45 96 99

BARQUETA DE BONITO

TUNA FISH BOATS

Ingredients: *Boat-shaped pastry cases, "Piquillo" red pepper, lettuce, tuna fish, onion, chili peppers, boiled prawns and mayonnaise.*

Method: Put some lettuce in the bottom of the pastry case and a chili pepper on top of it. Then a mixture of tuna fish with chili pepper, onion and mayonnaise. Garnish with a boiled prawn and little mayonnaise.

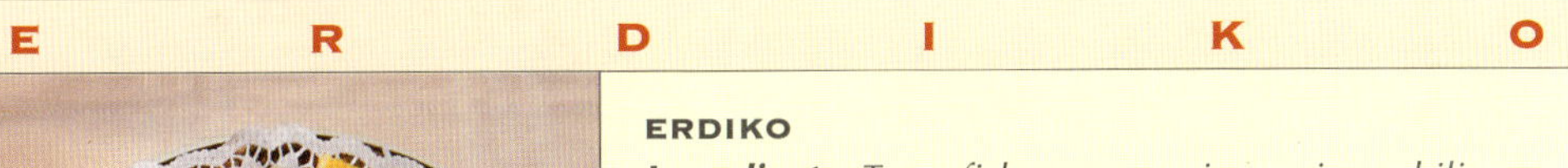

ERDIKO

ERDIKO

Ingredients: *Tuna fish, mayonnaise, onion, chili peppers and anchovies in oil.*

Method: Flake the tuna fish and chop the chili peppers and onion. Mix together and put some on to a piece of sliced bread. Garnish with two anchovy fillets one on each side with some pieces of chili pepper and mayonnaise in the middle.

SALMÓN

SALMON

Ingredients: *Burgos cheese (similar to "Ricotta"), smoked salmon, mayonnaise and "piquillo" pepper.*

Method: Cut the cheese the same size as some sliced bread, spread some mayonnaise on top of the cheese and then a slice of smoked salmon on top of that. Put some mayonnaise on the salmon and garnish with a piece of pepper.

JAMÓN CON ANCHOA

DELICIA MARINA

BROCHETA D
GAMBA

ERREKA

Baratzategi nº 25 • Tel.: 943-28 25 72

JAMÓN CON ANCHOA

SALMON WITH ANCHOVY

Ingredients: *Cured ham, mayonnaise, hard-boiled egg, anchovy and a piece of bread.*

Method: Put some ham on to a piece of bread and some mayonnaise on top. Then sprinkle on some grated hard-boiled egg white, followed by some grated hard-boiled egg yolk. Garnish with an anchovy placed lengthwise.

DELICIA MARINA

MARINE DELIGHT

Ingredients: *Crab sticks, mayonaise, hard-boiled egg, large prawn, and a piece of bread.*

Method: Finely chop the crab stick and mix with the mayonnaise. Spread on to the bread and sprinkle some grated hard-boiled egg white on top. Then do the same with the yolk and garnish with a large prawn placed lengthwise.

BROCHETA DE GAMBA

PRAWN KEBAB

Ingredients: *2 large prawns (raw), a thin slice of bacon, half a cheese slice (processed cheese for sandwiches), a strip of "Morron" pepper, breadcrumbs.*

Method: Spread out the slice of bacon. At one one put the cheese, then the pepper on top followed by the two prawns. Make into a roll and hold everything together with a cocktail stick making sure that it pierces the two prawns. Coat with breadcrumbs and fry in plenty of oil.

ENSALADILLA RUSA

TORTILLA DE PATATA

E S N A O L A

Moraza nº 13 • Tel.: 943-45 93 94

E N S A L A D I L L A R U S A

RUSSIAN SALAD

Ingredients: *Tuna fish, egg, potato, ham and mayonnaise.*

Method: Boil the eggs and potatoes. Chop up all the ingredients and mix with the mayonnaise. Serve cold on a slice of bread.

T O R T I L L A D E P A T A T A

POTATO OMELETTE

Ingredients: *Potato, egg, onion, green pepper and a clove of garlic.*

Method: Fry the potato together with the onion, the pepper and the garlic. Remove from the pan and mix with the beaten egg. Return to the pan and cook on both sides.

C R O I S S A N T D E C H A T K A

CRAB STICK CROISSANT

Ingredients: *Crab stick, mayonnaise and mini croissants.*

Method: Flake the crab sticks and mix with the mayonnaise. Use this mixture to fill the croissants and serve.

ETXALDE

AZPEITI

URRAKI

ETXALDE

Toribio Alzaga nº 7 • Tel.: 943-45 37 28

ETXALDE

Ingredients: *Boiled ham, crab stick, hard-boiled egg, boiled prawns, mayonnaise and sliced bread.*

Method: Remove the crust from the sliced bread and cut it into rectangles. Put half a slice of ham and 2 slices of hard-boiled egg on the bread. The finishing touch is some crab stick topped by the prawns and mayonnaise.

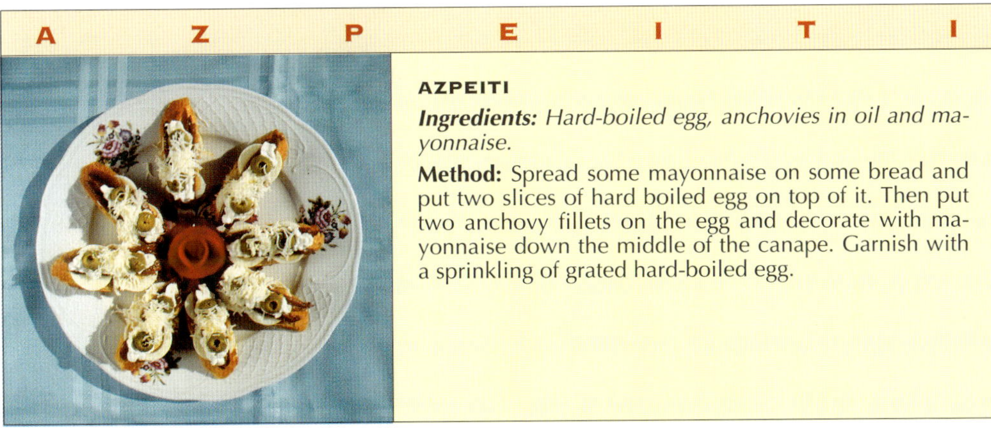

AZPEITI

Ingredients: *Hard-boiled egg, anchovies in oil and mayonnaise.*

Method: Spread some mayonnaise on some bread and put two slices of hard boiled egg on top of it. Then put two anchovy fillets on the egg and decorate with mayonnaise down the middle of the canape. Garnish with a sprinkling of grated hard-boiled egg.

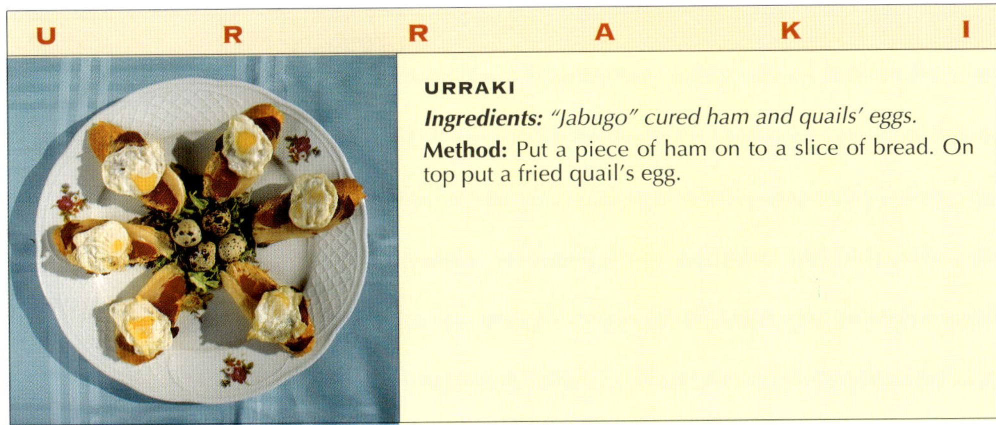

URRAKI

Ingredients: *"Jabugo" cured ham and quails' eggs.*

Method: Put a piece of ham on to a slice of bread. On top put a fried quail's egg.

BROTXETA

ROLLITO DE VERAN

BARCO DE
JAMÓN DE YORK

ETXANIZ

Fermin Calbeton nº 24 • Tel.: 943-42 62 59

BROTXETA

BACON AND PRAWN ROLLS

Ingredients: *Bacon and prawns.*

Method: Roll the prawns in a rasher of bacon and use a cocktail stick to hold everything together. Grill and serve on a slice of toasted bread.

ROLLITO DE VERANO

SUMMER ROLL

Ingredients: *Pork brawn, boiled ham, Russian salad, anchovy, red and green peppers, mayonnaise and chopped hard-boiled egg.*

Method: Put a slice of brawn on a piece of bread. Then on top put a roll of boiled ham with the Russian salad inside. Sprinkle some chopped hard-boiled egg on to the roll. Garnish the whole thing with strips of the peppers and anchovy. Top with a little mayonnaise.

BARCO DE JAMÓN DE YORK

HAM BOATS

Ingredients: *Chopped boiled ham, grated hard-boiled egg, salmon, mayonnaise, crispbread in the shape of a boat.*

Method: Mix the ham with the mayonnaise and spread it on to the crispbread. Sprinkle with some grated hard-boiled egg. Put a piece of salmon on top and garnish with a little mayonnaise.

ENSALADA ICIAR

PINTXO GABI

TRADICIONAL

GABI-ETXEA

Secundino Esnaola nº 39 • Tel.: 943-28 50 33

ENSALADA ICIAR

ICIAR SALAD

Ingredients: *Potato, tuna fish, tomato, onion, green pepper, oil and vinegar.*

Method: Boil the potato and dice it. Dice the tuna fish and slice the onion and tomato. Make the canape in this order: potato, tuna fish, tomato and onion. Dress with a vinaigrette made of oil, vinegar and chopped green pepper.

PINTXO GABI

GABI PINTXO

Ingredients: *Cod, green pepper, oil and bread.*

Method: Fry the cod together with the green pepper. Then serve on a slice of bread.

TRADICIONAL

TRADITIONAL

Ingredients: *Gherkin, tuna fish, anchovies in oil, stuffed olives, green peppers, oil and vinegar.*

Method: Cut the gherkins in half and put the tuna fish between the two halves. Hold everything together with a cocktail stick. Cover with an anchovy and finally an olive. Last of all dress with a vinaigrette made of oil, vinegar, and finely chopped pepper and onion.

ZUMAIA

HERNANI

TOLOSA

GANBARA

San Jerónimo nº 21 • Tel.: 943-42 25 75

Z U M A I A

ZUMAIA

Ingredients: *Crab sticks, mayonnaise, smoked salmon, sliced bread, lemon and onion.*

Method: Flake the crab sticks, mix with the mayonnaise and spread on the bread, leaving a small space for the smoked salmon. Garnish with some chopped onion, some drops of lemon juice and a little hot paprika.

H E R N A N I

HERNANI

Ingredients: *Potatoes, eggs, large carrots, tuna fish in oil, olives with their stones, red pepper, mayonnaise, salt, pepper, gherkin, oil, peas and prawns.*

Method: Boil the potatoes, eggs and carrots. Dice and add the salt and pepper. Then add finely chopped gherkin, olives and red pepper. After that put in the tuna fish, some peas, some mayonnaise and mix. Spread this salad onto pieces of bread and garnish with chopped egg and a prawn.

T O L O S A

TOLOSA

Ingredients: *Puff pastry and "chorizo" chipolata.*

Method: Cut the pastry into strips and wrap it round each small piece of chipolata. Glaze with beaten egg and bake in a hot oven (250°) until they have browned.

PASAIA

RENTERÍA

KOXKERO

P A S A I A

PASAIA

Ingredients: *Hake's roe, parsley, onion, salt, olive oil and wine vinegar.*

Method: Clean the roe and boil for 12-15 minutes with water, salt and a little vinegar. Cool. Attach a piece of onion to each piece of roe with a cocktail stick. Put them on a plate and dress with the wine vinegar, olive oil and chopped parsley.

R E N T E R Í A

RENTERIA

Ingredients: *"Piquillo" red peppers, anchovies in oil, gherkin, onion, edible fungi, olive oil, lemon, salt and garlic.*

Method: Put the peppers on a plate and add olive oil, salt and chopped garlic. Leave for a few minutes. Take a piece of toasted bread and on each one put the peppers, then 2 anchovy fillets, the gherkin, plus the onion and edible fungi both cut into thin (julienne) strips. Add a few drops of lemon juice and olive oil.

K O X K E R O

KOXKERO

Ingredients: *Prawns, parsley, salt, pepper, egg and flour.*

Method: Peel and season the prawns. Beat the egg to make a batter. Add a little chopped parsley to the egg. Put 2 or 3 prawns on to a cocktail stick, dip in flour and egg and fry over a medium heat until they have browned.

ROLLO RUSO

PINTXOS DEL CANTÁBRICO

PINTXOS DEL PESCADOR

G A N D A R I A S

31 de Agosto nº 25 • Tel.: 943-42 81 06

R O L L O R U S O

RUSSIAN ROLL

Ingredients: *Boiled ham, prawn, mayonnaise, a piece of bread, Russian salad (potato, carrot, peas, grated hard-boiled egg, mayonnaise and tuna fish in oil).*

Method: Cut a large slice of ham into 3 pieces. Spread a spoonful of Russian salad onto the ham and make the ham into a roll with the Russian salad inside. Spear a boiled prawn onto one end of a cocktail stick and use the other end to attach the ham roll to the bread. Garnish with mayonnaise along the length of the ham and grated hard-boiled egg.

P I N T X O S D E L C A N T Á B R I C O

CANTABRIAN PINTXOS

Ingredients: *Marinaded tuna fish, mayonnaise, grated lettuce, anchovy, grated hard-boiled egg and a slice of bread.*

Method: First mix the mayonnaise with the tuna fish and spread onto a piece of bread. Sprinkle with very finely chopped lettuce. Put an anchovy lengthwise on top. Grate some hard-boiled egg over it and put some mayonnaise on the anchovy.

P I N T X O S D E L P E S C A D O R

FISHERMAN´S PINTXOS

Ingredients: *3 anchovies in oil, slice of bread and vinaigrette (onion, parsley, oil, vinegar and salt).*

Method: Cut a long, thin slice of bread. Cover it with 3 anchovies. Serve with a little vinaigrette in the middle of the anchovies.

PINTXO DE HUEVO

PINTXO VERANIEGO

BACALAO AHUMADO

PINTXO DE HUEVO

EGG PINTXO

Ingredients: *Half an egg, prawn, mayonnaise, grated hard-boiled egg.*

Method: Cut a hard-boiled egg in half. Cut a small slice off the bottom so that it will not fall off the piece of bread. Decorate the top edges of the egg with mayonnaise. Spear a boiled prawn onto one end of a cocktail stick and push the other end through the egg as far as the bread. Garnish with grated hard-boiled egg.

PINTXO VERANIEGO

SUMMER PINTXO

Ingredients: *Slices of tomato, lettuce, boiled ham, anchovy in oil and seafood vinaigrette (tomato, egg, onion, green pepper, red pepper, egg white, salt, oil and vinegar).*

Method: Cut a generous slice of bread. Put a thin slice of tomato on top. Put a piece of boiled ham on top of that. Take an anchovy fillet and lay it across the ham. Add a little seafood vinaigrette to finish.

BACALAO AHUMADO

SMOKED COD

Ingredients: *Smoked cod, toasted bread, seafood vinaigrette (see above recipe).*

Method: Cut the crusts off the sliced bread, cut the slices in half and toast in the oven. Cover the slices completely with the smoked cod. Cover the slices with a thin film of vegetable oil and add the seafood vinaigrette.

TRONCOS DE ATÚN
CON GAMBAS

TARTALETA GAROA

IBÉRICOS

GAROA

Zabaleta nº 67 • Tel.: 943-27 71 04

TRONCOS DE ATÚN CON GAMBAS

TUNA FISH WITH PRAWNS

Ingredients: *Pickled tuna fish, prawns and olives.*

Method: Take a cocktail stick and spear a piece of tuna, a boiled peeled prawn and an olive on to it.

TARTALETA GAROA

GAROA TARTLET

Ingredients: *Pastry tartlet case, tuna fish, mayonnaise, boiled prawns and hard-boiled egg.*

Method: Chop up the tuna fish and the prawns, mix with mayonnaise and put the mixture in the pastry case. Garnish with grated hard-boiled egg.

IBÉRICOS

IBERIANS

Ingredients: *Egg and Iberian (cured) ham.*

Method: Boil the egg and cut it in half. Put one half of the egg on to a slice of cured ham. Hold together with a cocktail stick and garnish with mayonnaise and grated hard-boiled egg.

REVUELTO DE CHAMPIÑÓN

BACALAO ENCEBOLLADO

MOUSSE DE PIMIENTO

GAZTELU

31 de Agosto nº 22 • Tel.: 943-42 14 11

REVUELTO DE CHAMPIÑÓN

MUSHROOM SCRAMBLED EGG

Ingredients: *Button mushrooms, garlic, chili pepper, oil and salt.*

Method: Finely chop the mushrooms and put in an earthenware dish. Add finely chopped garlic and chili pepper and then the oil and salt. Cook until the mixture thickens and serve on a slice of bread.

BACALAO ENCEBOLLADO

COD WITH ONION

Ingredients: *Cod, onion, green pepper, olive oil, salt and "fumet" (concentrated fish stock).*

Method: Cut the onion and pepper into thin (julienne) strips. Put them to heat in an earthenware dish with the oil and a little salt. Cook gently and when they have softened sufficently, add the pieces of cod, pour over some "fumet" and bring to the boil. Serve the cod covered with the sauce.

MOUSSE DE PIMIENTO

RED PEPPER MOUSSE

Ingredients: *"Piquillo" red peppers, onion, cream, egg and a little pepper, if desired.*

Method: Cook the peppers with a little garlic, salt and sugar. In a separate earthenware dish gently fry the onion in oil. When the onion is soft add the peppers and pepper (if desired) and mix thoroughly. Blend and then strain in order to obtain a smooth sauce. In a separate bowl beat the eggs and cream and add the pepper puré. Mix thoroughly and cook in the oven bain marie for about 1 hour.

BACALAO CON PIMIENTOS

ALZADO DE JAMÓN

ENSALADILLA RUSA

G E L T O K I B I

Reyes Católicos nº 5 • Tel.: 943-45 08 84

B A C A L A O C O N P I M I E N T O S

COD WITH PEPPERS

Ingredients: *Fillets of cod with the salt removed, green pepper, onion, oil and cayenne pepper.*

Method: Gently fry the finely chopped pepper and onion in an earthenware dish. Then add the pieces of cod, sprinkle some cayenne pepper over them and allow to cook over a medium heat. Serve the cod on bread with the softened peppers and onions on top.

A L Z A D O D E J A M Ó N

HAM

Ingredients: *Green peppers, hard-boiled egg, Iberian (cured) ham and mayonnaise.*

Method: Cut the green pepper into small pieces and gently fry. Arrange on a piece of bread and put a slice of hard-boiled egg, some mayonnaise and the ham on top.

E N S A L A D I L L A R U S A

RUSSIAN SALAD

Ingredients: *Boiled potatoes, peas, hard-boiled egg, tuna fish, prawns and mayonnaise.*

Method: Dice all the ingredients and mix them with the mayonnaise. Spread the mixture on to a slice of bread and sprinkle with grated hard-boiled egg.

TXOPITO

FLOR DE SALMÓN

ROLLITO

T X O P I T O

BABY SQUID

Ingredients: *Squid, green pepper, red pepper, onion, hard-boiled egg, olives and tomato.*

Method: Chop the peppers, onion, egg, olives and tomato. Season and gently fry. Then add some pieces of thoroughly cleaned squid. Stuff the squid with this mixture, then dip them in flour and egg and fry. Blend the stuffing which is left over and use it as a garnish for the canape.

F L O R D E S A L M Ó N

SALMON FLOWERS

Ingredients: *Slice of bread, smoked salmon, red pepper, green pepper, kiwi fruit and onion.*

Method: Put a slice of smoked salmon on a piece of bread. On top put some finely chopped red and green pepper and onion plus a piece of kiwi fruit.

R O L L I T O

LITTLE ROLLS

Ingredients: *Boiled ham, cheese, bechamel sauce, small pieces of button mushroom and cured ham.*

Method: Prepare a light bechamel sauce with chopped mushroom and cured ham. When the sauce has cooled, wrap some in a slice of cheese and then in a slice of boiled ham. Dip in flour, egg and breadcrumbs and fry in plenty of hot oil. Serve hot.

ANCHOAS MARINADAS CON PIMIENTOS

TARTALETAS DE BONITO

BROCHETAS DE ANCHOA CON VINAGRETA

GIROKI

Beltran nº 4 • Tel.: 943-42 13 65

ANCHOAS MARINADAS CON PIMIENTOS

MARINADED ANCHOVIES WITH PEPPERS

Ingredients: *Anchovies, green peppers, hard-boiled egg. For the marinade: salt, lemon juice, vinegar and olive oil. For the vinaigrette: green pepper, red pepper and green chili pepper.*

Method: Marinade the anchovies ensuring that they are covered by the oil. Leave for 12 hours. Finely chop the green pepper, the red pepper and the chili pepper and use them to make the vinaigrette. Serving: put a piece of fried green pepper on a piece of bread, on top of that a slice of hard-boiled egg, then the anchovy and pour some vinaigrette on to the whole thing.

TARTALETAS DE BONITO

TUNA FISH TARTLETS

Ingredients: *Tuna fish in oil, onion, vinegar, mayonnaise, pastry cases, hard-boiled egg, boiled peeled prawns.*

Method: Flake the tuna fish. Add very finely chopped onion, vinegar and mayonnaise. Mix thoroughly. Fill the pastry cases with this mixture. Garnish with grated hard-boiled egg and a prawn.

BROCHETAS DE ANCHOA CON VINAGRETA

ANCHOVY KEBABS WITH VINAIGRETTE

Ingredients: *Anchovies, peeled boiled prawns, olives. For the vinaigrette: salt, olive oil, vinegar, green and red pepper, green chili pepper, onion and hard-boiled egg white.*

Method: Marinade the anchovies as in pintxo nº 1 above. Finely chop the ingredients for the vinaigrette and add the rest of the ingredients. Serve on a cocktail stick as follows: put a rolled anchovy in the middle, a prawn on each side and an olive at each end of the stick. Cover with vinaigrette.

TRIANGULITOS VEGETALES

SALPICÓN DE GAMBAS

GOIZ-ARGI

Fermin Calbetón nº 4 • Tel.: 943-42 52 04

PIMIENTO RELLENO DE BONITO

PEPPER STUFFED WITH TUNA FISH

Ingredients: *"Piquillo" pepper and pickled tuna fish mixed with onion.*

Method: Mix the tuna fish and onion with mayonnaise. Stuff the pepper with this mixture.

TRIANGULITOS VEGETALES

LITTLE VEGETABLE TRIANGLES

Ingredients: *Sliced bread, tomato, prawn, lettuce, mayonnaise, boiled ham and hard-boiled egg.*

Method: Dice the tomato and cut the ham into very small pieces. Grate the hard-boiled egg. Mix all the ingredients with the mayonnaise. Spread on to a slice of bread and garnish with a slice of tomato. Cut the bread into 4 pieces and put some lettuce, some mayonnaise and a prawn on top.

SALPICÓN DE GAMBAS

PRAWN COCKTAIL

Ingredients: *Gherkin, tomato, prawns, pineapple, crab sticks, lettuce and mayonnaise.*

Method: Chop the gherkins, the (tinned) tomato, the pineapple in syrup, the crab sticks and the boiled prawns. Add vinegar and olive oil and mix thoroughly. Put a lettuce leaf on a slice of toasted bread, then spread some of the mixture on top. Garnish with a boiled prawn and two dots of mayonnaise on each side.

PASTEL DE PESCADO
VOLOVANES DE REVUELTO DE SETAS Y GAMBAS
PIMIENTOS RELLENOS DE TXANGURRO

GURE ARKUPE

Iztingorra (Antiguo district) • Tel.: 943-21 15 09

PASTEL DE PESCADO

FISH CAKE

Ingredients: *4 fillets of fish (flaked), 6 eggs, white pepper, tomato ketchup, cream, salt and flaked spider crab.*

Method: Put all the ingredients in a bowl. Beat with an electric whisk and pour into a mould lined with butter and breadcrumbs. Cook in the oven bain marie at a temperature of 200°. When cooked turn it out of the mould and serve cold, garnished with mayonnaise.

PIMIENTOS RELLENOS DE TXANGURRO

PEPPERS STUFFED WITH SPIDER CRAB

Ingredients: *4 "piquillo" peppers, garlic, oil, parsley 1,500 g spider crab and half a litre of cocktail sauce.*

Method: Fry the peppers with garlic and allow to cool. Flake the spider crab and stuff the peppers with it. Arrange on a plate and cover with some cocktail sauce. Sprinkle with some chopped parsley.

VOLOVANES DE REVUELTO DE SETAS Y GAMBAS

MUSHROOM AND PRAWN VOL-AU-VENTS

Ingredients: *4 individual vol-au-vents, 500 g of mushrooms, 20 prawns, 8 eggs, oil and parsley.*

Method: Fry the mushrooms, prawns and parsley. When they are well-cooked, add the eggs and stir without allowing them to set completely. Before the mixture gets cold, use it to fill the vol-au-vents and serve hot.

PIMIENTOS RELLENO
DE BACALAO

TORTILLA DE ANCHOAS
CON AJOS FRESCOS

GURE-TXOKO

Usandizaga nº 5 • Tel.: 943-28 24 19

PIMIENTOS RELLENOS DE BACALAO

PEPPERS STUFFED WITH COD

Ingredients: *Cod with the salt removed, green peppers, onion, butter, flour, milk, 1 tin of "piquillo" peppers. For the sauce: garlic, leek, and a tin of "Morron" peppers.*

Method: Finely chop the onion and green peppers and gently fry in the butter together with the cod. Make a light bechamel sauce and add it to the cod and peppers. When the mixture has cooled, stuff the "piquillo" peppers with it. To make the sauce, gently fry all the ingredients and blend them into a sauce. Boil thoroughly and cover the peppers with it.

TORTILLA DE ANCHOAS CON AJOS FESCOS

ANCHOVY AND FRESH GARLIC OMELETTE

Ingredients: *Half a kilo of anchovies, a tray of fresh young garlic shoots, 6 eggs and salt.*

Method: Clean the anchovies and cut them into pieces. Cut the garlic into thin julienne strips and gently fry in plenty of oil. When they have browned add the anchovies, fry them gently and add some salt. Finally remove part of the oil, and add the eggs to make the omelette.

MOUSSE DE ESPÁRRAGOS

ASPARAGUS MOUSSE

Ingredients: *Onion, butter, a tin of asparagus, cream, 5 eggs and salt.*

Method: Finely chop the onion and fry it gently in the butter. Add a tin of asparagus with all the liquid and season. Let it boil a little and then pour it though a strainer. Mix with the eggs and cream (equal quantities of eggs and cream). Pour into a pudding mould and bake for 35 minutes bain marie.

LIBIAS

BACALAO
DOS SALSAS

BUÑUELOS DE
BACALAO

H A I Z E A

Aldamar nº 8 • Tel.: 943-42 57 10

L I B I A S

LIBIAS

Ingredients: *Oil, onion, garlic, brandy, white pepper, flaked spider crab and cocktail sauce.*

Method: Gently fry the garlic and onion in a little oil. Add brandy, white pepper and the spider crab. Season to taste. Keep on a low heat and then remove from the heat. As it cools add the cocktail sauce, which has been warmed up beforehand. Serve in crab shells with a sprinkling of chopped parsley.

B A C A L A O D O S S A L S A S

COD WITH TWO SAUCES

Ingredients: *Oil, fillets of cod with the salt removed, red and green peppers, onion, leek, garlic, parsley and salt.*

Method: Gently fry in a little oil the onion, leek, and the red and green peppers, which have been cut into thin strips. Separately prepare some straw potatoes by gently frying some thin slices of potato and adding some parsley and garlic. Cook the cod until the flakes start to separate. Put the flakes of cod onto the cooked potato and on top the straw potato with the fried onion, leek and peppers. Garnish with two sauces: one made with squid and the other with peppers.

B U Ñ U E L O S D E B A C A L A O

COD BUNDLES

Ingredients: *Oil, cod, onion, parsley, salt, white pepper, prawns and choux pastry.*

Method: Toss the cod, which has had the salt removed and has been flaked, in oil with very thinly sliced onion. When they are cooked add finely chopped prawns and the white pepper. Allow everything to cook. Mix with the choux pastry and plenty of chopped parsley. Season to taste and allow to cook. Make bundles with the mixture and fry.

HARITZA

PINTXO AZPEITIA

PINTXO INTXAURRONDO

H A R I T Z A

Triunfo nº 5 • Tel.: 943-46 93 75

H A R I T Z A

HARITZA

Ingredients: *Crab sticks, mayonnaise, strips of cured ham and smoked salmon in oil.*

Method: Chop the crab sticks and mix with the mayonnaise and spread the mixture onto a slice of bread to cover it completely. For salmon with crab sticks: bread with crab sticks and a garnish of strips of salmon. For crab sticks: bread with crab sticks, a little mayonnaise and a small strip of smoked salmon as a garnish, or strips of cured ham in a criss-cross design. Ham with salmon: Cover the bread with a slice of ham. Add a strip of salmon, then a slice of hard-boiled egg with some crab sticks.

P I N T X O   A Z P E I T I A

AZPEITIA PINTXO

Ingredients: *Pickled tuna fish, mayonnaise, chili peppers, tomato sauce and anchovies.*

Method: For all the variations of this canapé first flake the tuna fish. For the "El Rizo" variation spread some mayonnaise on a slice of bread, put some chopped tuna fish on top, a chili pepper on top of that and finally an anchovy. For the "Picado" variation chop some chili peppers, add a little vinegar and oil to moisten the mixture (with the flaked tuna fish) and garnish with an anchovy on top.

P I N T X O   I N T X A U R R O N D O

INTXAURRONDO PINTXO

Ingredients: *Very finely chopped salmon and cured ham, eggs, crab sticks, prawn paste, and Russian salad (olives, egg, potatoes, tuna fish and mayonnaise).*

Method: To make the prawn mousse version: blend the prawn paste and mix with the mayonnaise. Spread onto a slice of bread and garnish with a few prawns and a posy of mayonnaise. To make the Russian salad version: spread some Russian salad onto a slice of bread, covering it completely. Then put a slice of hard-boiled egg on top, followed by mayonnaise and plenty of grated hard-boiled egg. Garnish with something colourful like a slice of carrot.

TXAPELA
PASTEL DE MEJILLÓN
PASTEL DE PIMIENTOS

HEGO-ALDE

Virgen del Carmen nº 9 • Tel.: 943-27 72 82

TXAPELA

BASQUE BERETS

Ingredients: *Button mushrooms, prawns, garlic and mini-rusks.*

Method: Clean the mushrooms and use two caps for each Basque beret. Fry in very hot oil. Fry the prawns with garlic separately. Take a mini-rusk, put a fried mushroom top on it with the underside facing up, fill with the prawn and garlic mixture, and cover with another mushroom cap, with the underside facing down. Hold everything together with a cocktail stick.

PASTEL DE MEJILLÓN

MUSSEL PUDDING

Ingredients: *Mussels, green and red pepper, spring onion, 4 eggs, cream, margarine and salt.*

Method: Gently fry finely chopped onion and peppers. Mix with the boiled, chopped mussels. Beat the eggs and the cream and add to the mixture of mussels, onions and peppers. Season. Grease the inside of a mould with margarine, pour in the mixture and cook in the oven bain marie at 210° for an hour. Serve on sliced bread.

PASTEL DE PIMIENTOS

PEPPER PUDDING

Ingredients: *A tin of red peppers, 4 eggs, cream, salt and margarine.*

Method: With a high-speed whisk blend the red peppers, cream and eggs. Season. Grease the inside of a mould with margarine, pour the mixture into it and cook in the oven bain marie at 210° for an hour. Serve on sliced bread and garnish with red pepper and mayonnaise.

DELICIAS DEL MAR
EN VINAGRETA

BARQUITA DE ANCHOA

HONTZA

Plaza Baratzategi nº 28 • Tel.: 943-32 16 40

DELICIAS DEL MAR EN VINAGRETA

SEAFOOD DELIGHTS WITH VINAIGRETTE

Ingredients: *Prawns, crab sticks, boiled ham, sliced cheese, olives, red and green pepper, and onion.*

Method: Spear a prawn, the crab stick, a strip of ham interwoven with half a slice of cheese and an olive onto a cocktail stick. Pour some vinaigrette (made with red and green pepper and onion) over it.

BARQUITA DE ANCHOA

ANCHOVY BOATS

Ingredients: *Crispbread, sliced cheese, 2 slices of hard-boiled egg, 2 anchovies, black olives, pepper butter.*

Method: Arrange a slice of cheese and the slices of hard-boiled egg on the crispbread. Then add the olives with the anchovy fillets curled round them. Finally garnish with the pepper butter.

TROPICAL

TROPICAL

Ingredients: *Apple, pineapple, boiled chicken, hard-boiled egg, morello cherries, cocktail sauce and toasted bread.*

Method: Chop the apple, pineapple and chicken. Mix with the cocktail sauce. Put grated hard-boiled egg on top. Garnish with prawns and cherries and arrange everything on the toasted bread.

REVUELTOS DEL PIQUILLO CON ANCHOAS

SALMÓN CON HUEVO

ANCHOAS RELLENAS DE PIMIENTO

I D O I A

Avda Isabel II nº 6

REVUELTOS DEL PIQUILLO CON ANCHOAS

"PIQUILLO" PEPPERS WITH SCRAMBLED EGG

Ingredients: *"Piquillo" peppers, anchovies, garlic, olive oil, eggs, toasted bread and green pepper.*

Method: Finely chop the garlic and fry gently. Add the "piquillo" peppers cut into strips and when they have softened add the cleaned anchovies. When they are cooked, add the egg and mix thoroughly. Spread on a slice of toasted bread and garnish with a few strips of green pepper.

SALMÓN CON HUEVO

SALMON WITH EGG

Ingredients: *Toasted bread, salmon, egg, prawns and mayonnaise.*

Method: Put a slice of salmon on the toasted bread. On top of that put a slice of egg and cover with mayonnaise. Then put a boiled, peeled prawn and garnish with grated hard-boiled egg.

ANCHOAS RELLENAS DE PIMIENTO

ANCHOVIES STUFFED WITH PEPPERS

Ingredients: *Anchovies, green pepper, flour and egg.*

Method: Put a pepper between two anchovies as if it was a sandwich. Dip in flour and egg and fry in very hot oil.

BONITO CON TOMATE

IOSUNE

I O S U N E

Paseo de Zorroaga nº 15 • Tel.: 943-46 28 45

B O N I T O   C O N   T O M A T E

TUNA FISH WITH TOMATO

Ingredients: *Tuna fish, fresh tomato, hard-boiled egg, onion and a slice of fried bread.*

Method: Finely chop the egg and onion and mix well with the flaked tuna fish and tomato. Spread the mixture on to the slice of fried bread and garnish with grated hard-boiled egg.

I O S U N E

IOSUNE

Ingredients: *Boiled ham, mayonnaise, hard-boiled egg and a slice of bread.*

Method: Finely chop the boiled ham and egg and mix them with the mayonnaise. Spread on to a slice of bread.

T O R T I L L A   D E   B A C A L A O

COD OMELETTE

Ingredients: *Cod, onion, green pepper and egg.*

Method: Gently fry the finely chopped onion and pepper. Add the flaked, de-salted cod. When they are done add the eggs and make the omelette.

IKURRIÑA

ENSALADILLA "IRAETA"

TARTALETA DE GAMBAS

IRAETA

Padre Larroca nº 2 • Tel.: 943-27 29 73

IKURRIÑA

BASQUE FLAG

Ingredients: *Red pepper, chili pepper, mayonnaise, toasted bread, chopped tuna fish and anchovy.*

Method: Toast the bread. Put some flaked tuna fish on top. Garnish with an anchovy, red pepper, mayonnaise and chili pepper.

ENSALADILLA "IRAETA"

IRAETA SALAD

Ingredients: *Bread, lettuce, tomato, egg, boiled ham and mayonnaise.*

Method: Chop the hard-boiled egg and mix with a slice of ham, tomato, lettuce and mayonnaise. Spread onto a slice of bread.

TARTALETA DE GAMBAS

PRAWN TARTLETS

Ingredients: *Pastry, lettuce, prawns and cocktail sauce.*

Method: Prepare with pastry tartlets. Chop the boiled prawns together with the lettuce and then mix with the cocktail sauce. Fill the tartlets with this mixture.

ANCHOA VINAGRETA

GAMBA ROSA

VELERO

SAILING SHIP

Ingredients: *Boiled ham, bread, half a hard-boiled egg, Russian salad and boiled prawns.*

Method: Cover a piece of bread with a slice of ham and half a hard-boiled egg filled with Russian salad. Add a prawn to resemble a sail.

GAMBA ROSA

PINK PRAWN

Ingredients: *Sliced bread, lettuce, prawns and cocktail sauce.*

Method: Spread some mayonnaise onto a triangle of sliced bread. Cover with some chopped lettuce and two boiled prawns. Cover with cocktail sauce.

ANCHOA VINAGRETA

ANCHOVY WITH VINAIGRETTE

Ingredients: *Anchovies, vinegar, garlic, salt, red and green peppers, olive oil and tuna fish.*

Method: Put some anchovies in vinaigrette on a tray. Cover with finely chopped red and green pepper and tuna fish. Pour over some garlic fried in olive oil together with some of the oil used for frying.

SALMÓN

PIPERRADA
CON ANCHOAS

IBÉRICO

ITXAROPENA

Embeltrán nº 16 • Tel.: 943-42 45 76

SALMON

SALMON

Ingredients: *Smoked salmon, anchovies in oil, oil, vinegar, onion, parsley and bread.*

Method: Toast the bread and cut a slice of salmon to cover the bread completely. Put 2 anchovies and some vinaigrette down the middle.

PIPERRADA CON ANCHOAS

"PIPERADE" WITH ANCHOVIES

Ingredients: *Green peppers, "Morron" red peppers, fresh anchovies, oil, parsley, garlic, red chili pepper, vinegar and salt.*

Method: Clean the anchovies and remove the heads and backbone. Cover them with water and add a quarter of a litre of vinegar per kilo of anchovies and a handful of salt. Leave them for 24 hours and turn them over from time to time in the liquid. Fry the red and green peppers cut in half. First put the green pepper on the bread followed by the red pepper in strips. On each side put the anchovies and on top the garlic, red chili pepper, parsley and oil.

IBÉRICO

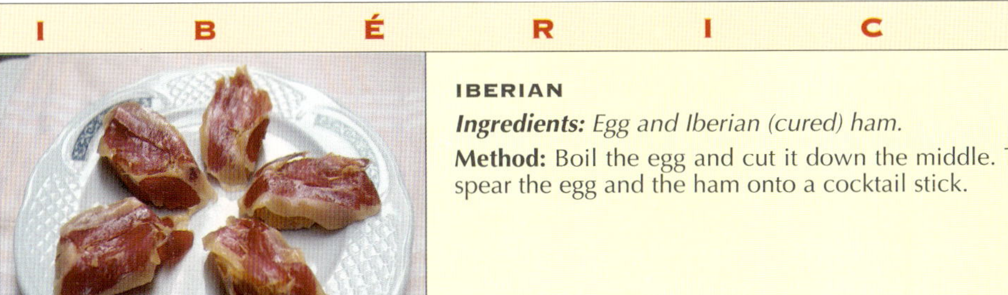

IBERIAN

Ingredients: *Egg and Iberian (cured) ham.*

Method: Boil the egg and cut it down the middle. Then spear the egg and the ham onto a cocktail stick.

VOLOVÁN ITXASKI

TORTILLA PRIMAVERA

TARTALETA MARINERA

I T X A S K I

Paseo Colón nº 12 • Tel.: 943-27 81 76

V O L O V Á N I T X A S K I

ITXASKI VOL-AU-VENT

Ingredients: *Butter, large prawns, black pepper, chopped parsley, salt. For the bechamel sauce (for 4 vol-au-vents): half a litre of milk, 3 level tablespoonfulls of flour, and 18 large prawns.*

Method: Beat the milk together with the flour. Melt the butter, add the chopped raw prawns and sprinkle with black pepper and chopped parsley. Fry gently, add the milk and flour mixture and allow to boil for about 20 minutes. Fill the vol-au-vents and serve hot.

T O R T I L L A P R I M A V E R A

SPRING OMELETTE

Ingredients: *Toasted sliced bread, a plain omelette, Emmental cheese, boiled ham, crab sticks, smoked salmon, cured ham (Iberian), hard-boiled egg, chopped prawn and mayonaise.*

Method: Cut all the ingredients into a circular shape. Using the sliced bread as a base arrange all the ingredients on top in the above order.

T A R T A L E T A M A R I N E R A

SAILOR'S TARTLET

Ingredients: *Smoked salmon, smoked trout, crab sticks, boiled potato, hard-boiled egg, peas, tuna fish, carrot and mayonnaise.*

Method: Mix all the ingredients, add the mayonnaise, mix everything thoroughly and put in the tartlet.

HOJALDRE RELLENO DE PUDÍN CON ANCHOAS

CHAMPIÑÓN ITXASPE

TOSTADITA ITXASPE

ITXASPE

Berminghan nº 17 • Tel.: 943-29 32 37

HOJALDRE RELLENO DE PUDÍN

PASTRY FILLED WITH ANCHOVY PUDDING

Ingredients: *Fish pudding, anchovy, crab sticks, tuna fish and one large prawn.*

Method: Mix the fish pudding with the anchovy, crab stick and tuna. Fill the pastry cases. Add a little mayonnaise and garnish with a prawn.

CHAMPIÑÓN ITXASPE

ITXASPE MUSHROOMS

Ingredients: *Button mushrooms, onion, pepper, garlic and a large prawn.*

Method: Gently fry the onion with the pepper and the garlic. Grill the mushroom cap. When it is cooked, fill with the fried onion, pepper and garlic and garnish with a peeled, grilled prawn.

TOSTADITA ITXASPE

ITXASPE TOAST

Ingredients: *Toasted bread, mayonnaise, smoked salmon, anchovies, large boiled prawn and vinaigrette.*

Method: Put a piece of salmon on the slice of toast. Put 2 anchovy filets and some vinaigrette on top. Then a boiled prawn and a little mayonnaise.

PINTXO DE BACALAO

PUDÍN DE CALABAZA

PIMIENTOS RELLENOS D TXANGURRO

I Z A Z P I

Paseo Baratzategi nº 33 (Intxaurrondo district)
Tel.: 943-27 92 18

PINTXO DE BACALAO

COD PINTXO

Ingredients: *Cod, green pepper, fresh tomato, onion and a chili pepper.*

Method: Flake the desalted cod. Gently fry chopped onion and green pepper. Add a couple of tablespoonfulls of tomato and a chili pepper. Then add the cod and cook gently. When the cod is cooked, fill the tartlets with the mixture. Garnish with boiled, peeled prawns and parsley.

PUDÍN DE CALABAZA

PUMPKIN PUDDING

Ingredients: *2 leeks, 3 boiled potatoes and a kilo of pumpkin.*

Method: Peel the pumpkin and boil in a large saucepan. Boil the potatoes and the leeks separately. When cooked, drain. Add the following to each of the 3 ingredients separately: 2 eggs, salt and ground white pepper. Grease the inside of a baking tin with butter. Pour the 3 mixtures into it in this order: first the pumpkin,then the leek and lastly the potato one. Bake in a hot oven for 20 minutes bain marie and serve with a roquefort cream.

PIMIENTOS RELLENOS DE TXANGURRO

PEPPERS STUFFED WITH SPIDER CRAB

Ingredients: *I spider crab weighting 1 kg, "piquillo" peppers and fresh tomato.*

Method: Boil the spider crab and flake the meat. Prepare a basic mixture of onion, carrot, leeks and garlic. Flambé it with brandy and blend it. Then mix this with the spider crab and a little red pepper. Stuff the peppers, dip in flour and fry. Then arrange in an earthenware dish. Add the tomato and allow to boil for 5 minutes.

PMIENTOS RELLENOS CON SALSA DE CHIPIRÓN

CHAMPIÑONES AL FOIE

BERZA RELLENA

PIMIENTOS RELLENOS CON SALSA DE CHIPIRÓN

PEPPERS STUFFED WITH SQUID SAUCE

Ingredients: *A tin of peppers, 1 black pudding weighing half a kilo, 2 sachets of squid ink and half a kilo of fresh tomato.*

Method: Finely chop some onion and cook gently. Skin and cut up the black pudding. Mix it with the onion and cook a little. When the mixture is cold, stuff the peppers with it. Dip them in flour and fry in hot oil. Then arrange in an earthenware dish. Add the squid ink and two tablespoonfulls of tomato. Boil for 5 minutes. Serve with fried bread if desired.

CHAMPIÑONES AL FOIE

BUTTON MUSHROOMS WITH LIVER PATE

Ingredients: *1/2 kilo of button mushrooms, 100 g of liver pâté and meat sauce.*

Method: Clean the mushrooms and cook with finely chopped onion for half an hour. When they are cooked, mix with the liver pate until it melts. Then add a little meat sauce made with marrow bone. Fill some tartlets with the mixture and serve.

BERZA RELLENA

STUFFED CABBAGE

Ingredients: *1 cabbage, 1/2 kilo of minced beef, one onion, 200 g of flour, a little butter and a litre of milk.*

Method: Clean the cabbage and boil the leaves whole. When they are cooked make a stuffing of minced beef, onion and a little bechamel sauce. When the mixture is cooked, stuff the leaves with it, and roll the leaves. Then dip the cabbage rolls in egg and fry. Arrange in an earthenware dish. Pour a light bechamel sauce over them and bake them "au gratin" for a little while in the oven.

CRÊPE RELLENO DE
KOKOTXAS IZEI

REVUELTO DE
GIBELURDIÑAS
CON LANGOSTINOS

PIMIENTO
RELLENO DE
CHIPIRÓN

IZEI

Paseo Baratzategi nº 22 • Tel.: 943-27 93 91

CRÊPE RELLENO DE KOKOTXAS IZEI

IZEI PANCAKES STUFFED WITH COD "KOKOTXAS"

Ingredients: *1 pancake (cooked in the traditional way), cod "kokotxas" (throats of the fish), "Pil-pil" sauce (made with oil, garlic and red chili pepper), Biscay sauce (made with dried spice peppers, onion and garlic).*

Method: Make a traditional round pancake. Cook half the kokotxas in the "pil-pil" sauce and the other half in the "Biscay" sauce. Stuff the pancake with the kokotxas. Mix the 2 sauces together thoroughly. Pour some on to a plate and arrange the pancake on top.

REVUELTO DE GIBELURDIÑAS

WILD FOREST MUSHROOM (RUSSULA) WITH EGG

Ingredients: *Wild forest mushrooms, pastry, large prawns, eggs, cream and quails' eggs.*

Method: Finely chop the large prawns and mushrooms and sauté in oil. Add an egg and a little cream and allow to set a little. Pour the mixture into a pastry case and decorate with prawn tails and hard-boiled quails' eggs.

PIMIENTO RELLENO DE CHIPIRÓN

PEPPER STUFFED WITH SQUID

Ingredients: *"Piquillo" peppers, squid in ink, "Biscay" sauce, bechamel sauce and spring onion.*

Method: Chop the squid cooked in its ink, thicken with a little bechamel sauce. Stuff the peppers with this mixture. Cover the outer part of the plate with the "Biscay" sauce and the inner part with the squid sauce. Put a stuffed pepper in the middle and garnish with the spring onion.

LANGOSTINO
VINAGRETA
PASTEL
KRABARROK
HUEVAS A LA
VINAGRETA

IZKIÑA

Euskadi Etorbidea nº 19 (Trincherpe district)
Tel: 943-39 90 43

LANGOSTINO VINAGRETA

LARGE PRAWNS WITH VINAIGRETTE

Ingredients: *Olive oil, vinegar, onion, garlic, parsley, red and/or green pepper, large prawn tails.*

Method: Boil the prawn tails in salted water for 5 minutes (according to size). Peel and prepare the vinaigrette with the rest of the ingredients.

PASTEL KRABARROKA

ROCK FISH PUDDING

Ingredients: *For a litre-sized mould : 1 rock fish weighing about 1 kg, 1/2 litre of cream and 1/2 a little home-made tomato sauce, 7 eggs, breadcrumbs and butter to grease the inside of the mould, salt and white pepper.*

Method: Cook the fish for 10 minutes in boiling water. Allow to cool, remove the bones and flake. Beat the eggs and mix with the rest of the ingredients including the fish. Put the mixture into the mould lined with the butter and breadcrumbs and bake in the oven bain marie for about 90 minutes.

HUEVAS A LA VINAGRETA

HAKE ROES WITH VINAIGRETTE

Ingredients: *Hake roes and vinaigrette ingredients as in the first recipe on this page.*

Method: Bring to the boil some water with salt, oil and half an onion. Put the roes into the boiling water and cook over a low heat so that they don't burst. Boil for 30 minutes.

PINTXO TRINTXERPE

SALMÓN

TARTALETA DE TXANGURRO

PINTXO TRINTXERPE

TRINTXERPE PINTXO

Ingredients: *Anchovies, vinegar, salt. For the sauce: olive oil, garlic, green pepper, red pepper and parsley.*

Method: To whiten the anchovies remove the bones and cover with salt and vinegar for 2 hours. Then rinse them and leave to drain. Prepare the sauce by gently frying chopped garlic and peppers in oil for 5 minutes. Then spread the anchovies out on a tray and pour the sauce over them.

SALMÓN

SALMON

Ingredients: *Smoked salmon, toasted bread, chopped onion.*

Method: Toast some slices of bread and on each piece put a slice of smoked salmon with some chopped onion on top.

TARTALETA DE TXANGURRO

SPIDER CRAB TARTLET

Ingredients: *Boiled spider crab, mayonnaise, pastry cases and lettuce.*

Method: Boil the spider crab for 15 minutes (for a 1 kg spider crab), remove the meat and break it up. Mix the crab meat with mayonnaise and lettuce cut into thin julienne strips. Fill the pastry cases with this mixture.

PIQUILLOS
RELLENOS
DE MORCILL

GILDAS JAI

ROSAS DE
ALEJANDRÍ

JAI ALAI

Ategorrieta nº 41 • Tel: 943-29 01 10

PIQUILLOS RELLENOS DE MORCILLA

PEPPERS STUFFED WITH BLACK PUDDING

Ingredients: *"Piquillo" peppers, black pudding from Villarcayo, onion, dried red spice peppers, tomato, parsley, cinnamon and bread.*

Method: Bake the peppers in the oven and remove the skins. Then remove the contents of the black pudding from the skin. Gently fry some finely chopped onion. Add the flesh of the dried spice pepper, the ground cinnamon and then the black pudding. Then stuff the peppers with this mixture. Dip them in flour and egg and fry. Serve on a slice of bread and garnish with a sauce made of dried spice pepper and tomato. Sprinkle a little chopped parsley on top.

GILDAS JAI

JAI CHILI PEPPERS

Ingredients: *Local chili peppers, fresh anchovy fillets in brine, olives stuffed with anchovy, and vinaigrette made with capers.*

Method: Spear a pepper, then a fresh anchovy fillet, and finally an olive on to a cocktail stick. Serve covered with a vinaigrette made with capers.

ROSAS DE ALEJANDRÍA

ROSES OF ALEXANDRIA

Ingredients: *Salmon marinaded with dill, hard-boiled egg, mayonnaise, caviar, pastry cases and fresh spring onion.*

Method: Put some mayonnaise round the edge of the pastry case and cover with grated hard-boiled egg yolk. Inside the tartlet put the white of the hard-boiled egg without the yolk. In the space where the yolk was put a little finely chopped spring onion and then some salmon, which is moulded into the shape of a rose. Garnish with a little caviar and sprinkle a little lemon juice over them.

PIMIENTOS
"ALAITZ"

BARQUETA
"JAIZKIBEL"

MORCILLA
"URKO"

JAIZKIBEL

Autonomía nº 9 • Tel: 943-45 83 72

PIMIENTOS "ALAITZ"

"ALAITZ" PEPPERS

Ingredients: *"Piquillo" peppers, tomato, cream, cod, onion, green pepper, flour and milk.*

Method: Make a light bechamel sauce with the flour, milk and cod. Fill the peppers with this sauce. Make the accompanying sauce with the peppers, tomato and cream.

BARQUETA "JAIZKIBEL"

"JAIZKIBEL" BOATS

Ingredients: *Crab sticks, mayonnaise, bread, salmon, onion, large prawns and cocktail sauce.*

Method: Mix the crab sticks cut into small pieces with the cocktail sauce and put in the middle of the bread. Mix the salmon with the chopped onion and mayonnaise. Cover the rest of the bread with this mixture. Garnish with a strip of salmon and a boiled prawn in the middle.

MORCILLA "URKO"

"URKO" BLACK PUDDING

Ingredients: *Black pudding from Eibar and lettuce.*

Method: Boil the black pudding over a very low heat and serve on a bed of lettuce.

ENDIBIA

SALMÓN

HUEVO

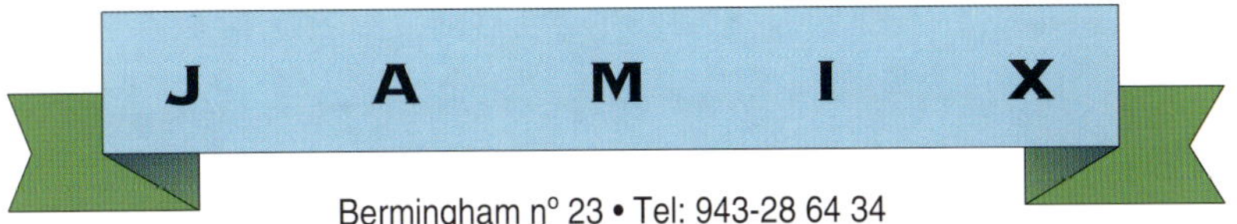

JAMIX

Bermingham nº 23 • Tel: 943-28 64 34

ENDIBIA

CHICORY

Ingredients: *Chicory (Belgian endive), tuna fish with mayonnaise, stuffed olives, anchovies in oil and bread.*

Method: Put a chicory leaf on a slice of bread and fill it with the tuna fish mixed with mayonnaise. Garnish with a stuffed olive and an anchovy fillet, as in the photo.

SALMÓN

SALMON

Ingredients: *Fried bread, cured ham, smoked salmon, hard-boiled egg and prawns.*

Method: Put a slice of cured ham on a piece of fried bread. Put a slice of smoked salmon on top, followed by a slice of hard-boiled egg and a little mayonnaise. Garnish with a boiled prawn.

HUEVO

EGG

Ingredients: *Toasted bread, hard-boiled egg, anchovies in oil, boiled prawns and mayonnaise.*

Method: Toast the bread and place an anchovy fillet on top. On top of that put half a hard-boiled egg and some mayonnaise. Garnish with some grated hard-boiled egg and a boiled prawn.

ESPECIAL

PASTEL DE PESCADO

BIERZO

J O S E   M A R I

Fermin Calbetón nº 5 • Tel: 943-42 46 45

E S P E C I A L

SPÉCIAL

Ingredients: *Lettuce cut into thin julienne strips, boiled prawns, cocktail sauce and chopped hard-boiled egg.*

Method: Make a cocktail sauce with mayonnaise, tabasco sauce, Worcester sauce, brandy and a little home-made tomato sauce. Spread some of the sauce onto a slice of bread. Put a prawn at each end and the lettuce in the middle. Cover with more cocktail sauce and sprinkle with chopped egg.

P A S T E L   D E   P E S C A D O

FISH CAKE

Ingredients: *Onion, green pepper, homemade tomato sauce, hake, eggs and cream.*

Method: Gently fry the onion and green pepper. Add the hake in pieces, cook thoroughly and season. Blend with a high-speed whisk and add the tomato sauce, cream and eggs. Pour the mixture into a mould lined with butter and breadcrumbs. Bake in the oven bain marie for 40 minutes.

B I E R Z O

BIERZO

Ingredients: *Boiled ham, gherkin, crab stick, prawn, mayonnaise and cocktail sauce.*

Method: Cut everything into thin julienne strips and mix with the mayonnaise. Spread the mixture onto a slice of bread and on top put some cocktail sauce (made as in the first canape on this page). Garnish with a peeled prawn on the sauce.

FOIE A LA MANZANA

MILHOJAS DE BACALAO

REVUELTO DE HONGOS CON FOIE FRESCO

JOXEAN

Secundino Esnaola nº 41 • Tel: 943-28 06 44

FOIE A LA MANZANA

LIVER WITH APPLE

Ingredients: *Stewed apples (pippin apple, water, sugar, cinnamon), liver, raspberry sauce (burnt sugar, sweet wine, meat stock, raspberry vinegar and raspberry jam).*

Method: Put some stewed apple on a plate. Cut the liver into thin slices and season. Then grill them turning them over continually. Put the slices of grilled liver on the stewed apple and pour the raspberry sauce round it.

MILHOJAS DE BACALAO

COD SLICE

Ingredients: *Desalted cod, potatoes, red "piquillo" pepper, onion, garlic, parsley, salt, meat stock, leek, carrot and onion.*

Method: Prepare some potatoes a la "boulangère" in a frying pan with oil, salt, garlic and parsley. When the potatoes are cooked, arrange them in the middle of a plate. Boil and flake the cod. Put the cod flakes on the potato to form a "mountain". Then cook the onion, leek, carrot and potato cut into thin julienne strips by frying them in very hot oil. Then put the vegetables on the cod and surround the canape with a sauce made of peppers.

REVUELTO DE HONGOS CON FOIE FRESCO

SCRAMBLED EGG WITH EDIBLE FUNGI AND FRESH LIVER

Ingredients: *Edible fungi, onion, garlic, parsley, fresh liver and egg.*

Method: Finely chop and gently fry the onion. Cook the fungi with the onion and add garlic, parsley and salt. When the fungi are done add some chunks of fresh liver and the egg to make scrambled egg. Serve on a slice of toasted bread.

XIXAS CON HABAS Y
HUEVOS DE CODORNIZ

CHIPIRÓN
ENCEBOLLADO

PIMIENTO VERDE, RELLENO Y HOJALDRADO

STUFFED GREEN PEPPERS IN PASTRY

Ingredients: *Green pepper, carrot, onion, leek, minced fillet steak, cream and black pepper. For the base: pastry, mushrooms, garlic, parsley and cream.*

Method: To make the filling finely chop the leek, carrot and onion and gently fry them in oil until thoroughly cooked. Add some minced fillet steak and mix well. Use this mixture to stuff the green peppers, which have been grilled. Wrap the peppers in pastry, glaze with egg and cook in the oven. Serve on a mushroom and cream sauce.

XIXAS CON HABAS Y HUEVOS DE CODORNIZ

CHANTERELLE MUSHROOMS WITH QUAILS' EGGS

Ingredients: *Chanterelle mushrooms, broad beans, quails' eggs, garlic, parsley and salt.*

Method: Cook the mushrooms in a little oil wih garlic, parsley and salt. Boil the broad beans separately and when cooked mix with the mushrooms. Serve on a plate with a fried quail's egg on top.

CHIPIRÓN ENCEBOLLADO

SQUID WITH ONION

Ingredients: *Squid, onion, green pepper, oil, garlic and parsley.*

Method: Clean the squid and grill with a little oil until thoroughly browned. Chop the onion and pepper and fry gently. Then pour this mixture over the squid.

LANGOSTINOS DE TAFALLA

PINTXO TUCHO

JUAN SEBASTIAN BAR

Easo nº 7 • Tel.:943-42 30 66

LANGOSTINOS DE TAFALLA

"PRAWNS" OF TAFALLA

Ingredients: *Chili peppers, anchovies in oil and olives stuffed with anchovy.*

Method: Put 2 chili peppers, one anchovy and an olive on to a cocktail stick. Garnish with a vinaigrette sauce if desired.

PINTXO TUCHO

"TUCHO" PINTXO

Ingredients: *Small croissants, boiled ham, cheese and "chorizo" sausage from Salamanca.*

Method: Open the croissants down the middle and fill some with sausage and others with ham and cheese.

TORTILLA ESPAÑOLA

SPANISH OMELETTE

Ingredients: *Potatoes, eggs and oil.*

Method: Fry the potatoes in oil. When they are golden brown, remove them from the pan and mix with beaten eggs. Return the mixture to the pan to make an omelette, which should not be allowed to get too dry. Cut into portions and serve.

ANCHOA
JUANTXO
TARTALETA
DE CHAMPIÑÓN
TORTILLA
RELLENA

J U A N T X O

Embeltrán nº 6 • Tel.: 943-42 74 05

A N C H O A   J U A N T X O

JUANTXO ANCHOVIES

Ingredients: *Fresh anchovies, vinegar, red pepper, green pepper, carrot, salt and a piece of bread.*

Method: Marinade the anchovies in vinegar and salt for 24 hours. Then arrange on the bread and put strips of the red and green peppers on top. Garnish with grated raw carrot.

T A R T A L E T A   D E   C H A M P I Ñ Ó N

MUSHROOM TARTLET

Ingredients: *Button mushrooms, egg, salt, oil, pastry cases and parsley.*

Method: Wash and chop the mushrooms. Cook in oil with garlic for 10 minutes. Add the egg to make scrambled egg with the mushrooms and garlic. Fill the pastry cases with this mixture.

T O R T I L L A   R E L L E N A

STUFFED OMELETTE

Ingredients: *Potato omelette, lettuce, tomato, mayonnaise and bread.*

Method: Cut the omelette in half horizontally and fill with the lettuce, tomato and mayonnaise. Then cut into portions and serve on a piece of bread.

ROLLITO JULI

ENSALADA DE VERDURAS

BACALAO

J U L I

Moraza nº 11 • Tel.: 943-46 37 08

R O L L I T O J U L I

JULI ROLL

Ingredients: *Boiled ham, cheese and vegetables.*

Method: Roll all the chopped vegetables plus the cheese in the boiled ham and fry in hot oil.

E N S A L A D A D E V E R D U R A S

VEGETABLE SALAD

Ingredients: *Lettuce, seafood, green pepper, mayonnaise and bread.*

Method: Chop all the ingredients, mix with the mayonnaise and spread on the bread. Garnish with hard-boiled egg and prawn, as in the photo.

B A C A L A O

COD

Ingredients: *Green pepper, cod and onion.*

Method: Wrap the cod in the green pepper and dip in flour and egg. Fry in hot oil. Serve on a slice of bread and garnish with strips of fried onion.

LANGOSTIN
SALSA ROS

BACALAO

KEEPER

KEEPER

San Martin nº 49 • Tel.: 943-45 66 56

LANGOSTINO SALSA ROSA

LARGE PRAWN COCKTAIL

Ingredients: *Large fresh prawn, cocktail sauce and sliced bread.*

Method: Boil the prawns. Toast the sliced bread and cut into circles with a pastry cutter or a glass. Put a prawn on the circle of toast and garnish with cocktail sauce.

BACALAO

COD

Ingredients: *Fillets of fresh cod, flour, egg and bread.*

Method: Season the cod fillets and dip in flour and egg. Fry in hot oil and serve hot.

KEEPER

KEEPER

Ingredients: *Fresh anchovies, green peppers, red pepper, onion, oil, vinegar and toasted bread.*

Method: Blanch the anchovies and remove the backbone from the fillets. Put in a dish. Gently fry finely chopped green pepper, red pepper and onion in oil on a low heat to release the juices. Sprinkle with vinegar and mix with the anchovies.

BACALAO ENCEBOLLADO

KUKURRUKU

MEJILLONES RELLENOS

KUKURRUKU

San Lorenzo nº 5 • Tel.: 943-42 12 51

BACALAO ENCEBOLLADO

COD WITH ONION

Ingredients: *Desalted cod, green pepper, onion and olive oil.*

Method: Cut the onion and green pepper into thin julienne strips and gently fry in olive oil on a low heat. Then add the cod cut into pieces and fry on a low heat in the onion and green pepper sauce.

KUKURRUKU

KUKURRUKU

Ingredients: *Fresh anchovies, little green peppers from Gernika, egg and flour.*

Method: Clean the anchovies. Take a pepper, which has been fried over a very low heat, and place it between 2 anchovies. Dip into flour and egg and fry in very hot oil.

MEJILLONES RELLENOS

STUFFED MUSSELS

Ingredients: *Mussels, onion, red pepper, flour, milk, butter and tomato.*

Method: Clean the mussels thoroughly, boil and remove from the shells. Finely chop the onion, pepper and boiled mussels. Put in a saucepan with olive oil and allow to cook over a low heat. When cooked fill the shells with this mixture and cover with bechamel sauce.

KUPELA

ARAOZ

K U P E L A

José María Salaberría nº 3 • Tel.: 943-45 73 09

K U P E L A

KUPELA

Ingredients: *Toasted bread, hard-boiled egg, anchovies and mayonnaise.*

Method: Put a slice of hard-boiled egg onto the toast. Then put two anchovies lengthwise and cover the gap between them with mayonnaise. Garnish with grated hard-boiled egg.

A R A O Z

ARAOZ

Ingredients: *Bread, cured ham, red "piquillo" peppers, green pepper, anchovies in oil, hard-boiled egg and mayonnaise.*

Method: Put a slice of ham on a piece of bread. Put the sliced egg on the ham and the preen pepper on top of the egg, followed by the red pepper and the anchovies. Garnish by covering the edges with mayonnaise.

U R B A S A

URBASA

Ingredients: *Toasted bread, cured ham, crab stick, boiled prawn and mayonnaise.*

Method: Put a slice of ham on the toasted bread followed by the crab stick and the boiled prawn. Add some light mayonnaise.

ANCHOAS MARINADAS

PIMIENTOS RELLENOS DE CARNE

ENSALADA RUSA

K U R S A L

Zurriola nº 22 • Tel.: 943-29 11 50

ANCHOAS MARINADAS

MARINADED ANCHOVIES

Ingredients: *Fresh anchovies, salt, vinegar, onion, garlic and parsley.*

Method: Clean the anchovies and remove the backbone. Marinade in vinegar for 24 hours. Then arrange in a dish and cover with oil. Garnish with very finely chopped onion, garlic and parsley.

PIMIENTOS RELLENOS DE CARNE

PEPPERS STUFFED WITH MEAT

Ingredients: *Peppers, onion, parsley, meat, tomato, white wine and liver pâté.*

Method: Cook the meat and cut it into very small pieces. Mix with a little liver pâté and white wine. Allow the mixture to reduce a little and then stuff the peppers with it. Pour over some tomato sauce, which has been prepared beforehand.

ENSALADA RUSA

RUSSIAN SALAD

Ingredients: *Potatoes, hard-boiled eggs, peas, carrot, tuna fish and mayonnaise.*

Method: Boil the potatoes, eggs and carrot. Then chop thoroughly and mix with the tuna fish, peas and mayonnaise. Garnish to taste with grated hard-boiled egg, prawn etc.

DELICIAS
CESTA
TARTALETA
DE BACALA

LA ESPIGA

San Marcial nº 48 • Tel.: 943-42 142 33

DELICIAS

DELIGHTS

Ingredients: *Bread, anchovies, vinaigrette, mayonnaise and hard-boiled egg.*

Method: Put 2 anchovy fillets along each side of a piece of bread and some mayonnaise down the middle. Put half a slice of hard-boiled egg on top and a good vinaigrette on each side to finish.

CESTA

BASKETS

Ingredients: *Bread, onion, tuna fish, prawn, egg, anchovy and mayonnaise.*

Method: Prepare a salad with the hard-boiled egg, the tuna fish in oil and the onion. Put on some bread and then garnish with a chopped prawn, an anchovy and grated hard-boiled egg yolk.

TARTALETA DE BACALAO

COD TARTLET

Ingredients: *Flaked cod, "morron" red pepper, boiled potato, onion, garlic and cayenne pepper.*

Method: Gently fry the onion, garlic and chopped pepper. Add the flaked cod and allow to cook for 10 minutes. Mix with the potato cut into cubes and fill the tartlets with this mixture.

MORROS DE TERNERA
EN SALSA

FRITOS DE
LA ESPIGA

ANCHOAS GETARIA

GETARIA ANCHOVIES

Ingredients: *Fresh anchovies, oil, vinegar, salt, chili pepper and garlic.*

Method: Marinade the whole anchovies in vinegar and salt for 2 hours. Then open the anchovies and separate the fillets from the rest. Put the fillets in a dish and cover with fried garlic and chilli pepper.

MORROS DE TERNERA EN SALSA

CALVES' MUZZLES IN SAUCE

Ingredients: *Calves' muzzles, carrot, onion, garlic, white wine, egg, flour and salt.*

Method: Clean and boil the muzzles. Then cut and fry in batter. Prepare a sauce with the onion, carrot, garlic and white wine. When the sauce is cooked, add the fried muzzles.

FRITOS DE LA ESPIGA

ESPIGA FRITTERS

Ingredients: *This consists of a variety of different fritters, each one cooked in a different way. The following is a selection of some of the recipes.*

Method: Prawn in batter, brains, and ham mixed with hard-boiled egg are dipped in an Orly batter and fried. The "Milanaise" is made with boiled ham and cheese and fried in breadcrumbs. The stuffed pepper is made by filling a "piquillo" pepper with a bechamel sauce containing meat and button mushrooms. This is then fried in an Orly batter.

PINTXO
PRIMAVERA

PINTXO
EASO

LA HABANA

Easo nº 31 • Tel.: 943-43 03 35

TORTILLA LA HABANA

LA HABANA OMELETTE

Ingredients: *Potato omelette, crab stick, lettuce, mayonnaise and caviar.*

Method: Cut the omelette open horizontally in half and fill with crab stick, lettuce and mayonnaise. Garnish with a little mayonnaise and caviar.

PINTXO PRIMAVERA

SPRING PINTXO

Ingredients: *Sliced bread, smoked salmon, boiled ham and mayonnaise.*

Method: Mix the chopped ham and salmon with the mayonnaise. Spread onto a slice of bread and garnish the top with mayonnaise and salmon.

PINTXO EASO

EASO PINTXO

Ingredients: *Tuna fish in oil, mayonnaise, hard-boiled egg and anchovies.*

Method: Mix the tuna fish with the mayonnaise and spread on to a piece of sliced bread. Garnish with an anchovy with grated hard-boiled egg on top.

MARE NOSTRUM

EUSKAL PINTXO

HUEVO TODOS LOS SANTOS

LA TABERNA

Easo nº 7 • Tel.: 943-42 98 51

MARE NOSTRUM

MARE NOSTRUM

Ingredients: *Tuna fish in oil, raw onion, mayonnaise, green pepper and olives stuffed with anchovies.*

Method: Finely chop the onion and mix with the flaked tuna fish and mayonnaise. Spread onto a slice of bread and garnish with some strips of green pepper and a stuffed olive.

EUSKAL PINTXO

BASQUE PINTXO

Ingredients: *Boiled potato, peas, carrot, boiled monkfish, mayonnaise, hard-boiled egg, green and red pepper.*

Method: Chop the potato, carrot and monkfish and mix with the peas and mayonnaise. Spread onto a piece of bread. Garnish with a slice of hard-boiled egg and strips of green and red pepper.

HUEVO TODOS LOS SANTOS

ALL SAINTS' EGGS

Ingredients: *Hard-boiled egg, tuna fish in oil, mayonnaise, green pepper, red pepper, carrot and olives.*

Method: Spear a slice of carrot and an olive onto a cocktail stick. Then put half a hard-boiled egg onto the stick and garnish with mayonnaise along the length of the canape, some tuna fish and some very thin strips of peppers.

CRUZADO

TORPEDO

ROQUEFORT

L A N P E R N A

Igarabidea nº 19 • Tel.: 943-21 97 40

C R U Z A D O

CROSSES

Ingredients: *Toasted bread, green pepper, hard-boiled egg, anchovies in oil, boiled prawns and mayonnaise.*

Method: On a piece of toasted bread put a green pepper, a slice of hard-boiled egg, 2 anchovies and a prawn. Garnish with mayonnaise.

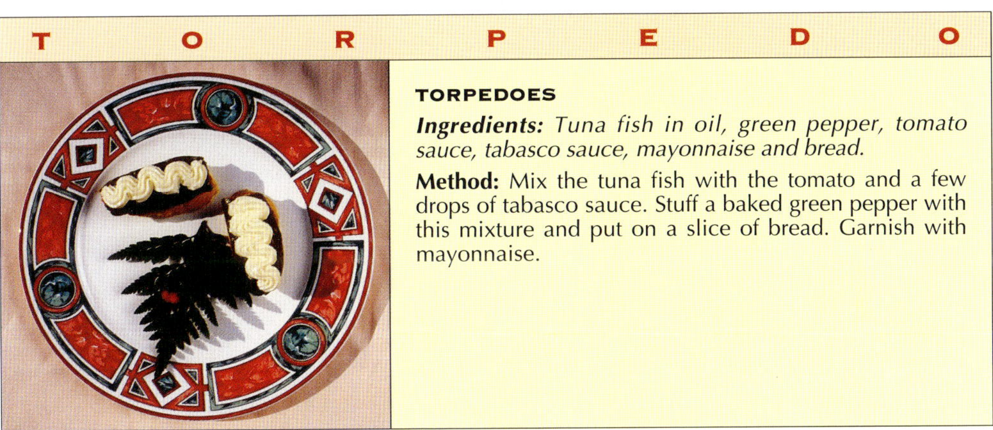

T O R P E D O

TORPEDOES

Ingredients: *Tuna fish in oil, green pepper, tomato sauce, tabasco sauce, mayonnaise and bread.*

Method: Mix the tuna fish with the tomato and a few drops of tabasco sauce. Stuff a baked green pepper with this mixture and put on a slice of bread. Garnish with mayonnaise.

R O Q U E F O R T

ROQUEFORT

Ingredients: *Blue cheese, cream, toasted bread, walnuts.*

Method: Mix the cheese with the cream and spread onto the some slices of toasted bread. Garnish with walnuts.

PIMIENTOS
RELLENOS
DE CHIPIRÓN

MONTADOS DE
ANCHOA

L A R R A

Juan de Bilbao • Tel.: 943-42 08 39

PIMIENTOS RELLENOS DE CHIPIRÓN

PEPPERS STUFFED WITH SQUID

Ingredients: *1 kg of fresh button mushrooms, 2 onions, 1 green pepper, 3 leeks, 2 tomatoes, salt and oil.*

Method: Clean the squid, chop and brown in a pan together with the vegetables and add a glass of white wine. When they are cooked, remove the squid, and add a very thin bechamel sauce to the squid and use this mixture to stuff the peppers. In the meantime strain the vegetables and add the squid ink. Put the peppers in the sauce and allow to cook gently for 15 minutes.

MONTADOS DE ANCHOA

MOUNTED ANCHOVIES

Ingredients: *Garlic, onion, "morron" red pepper, green pepper, fresh anchovies and salt.*

Method: Clean the anchovies and remove the heads and bones. Cover with vinegar and leave for 3 hours. In the meantime finely chop the onion, peppers and garlic. Put the anchovies in a dish one by one. Sprinkle them with salt and spread the chopped vegetables on top.

MERLUZA

HAKE

Ingredients: *Hake, salt, oil, flour and egg.*

Method: Season the hake and dip in flour and beaten egg. Fry in hot oil.

SERRANITO

MORCILLA EN HOJA DE BERZA

VOLOVÁN DE MANOS DE CERDO

LAS TABLAS

Salud nº 2 • Tel.: 943-46 52 15

SERRANITO

SERRANITO

Ingredients: *Iberian cured ham and bread.*

Method: Cut 2 very thin rectangular-shaped slices of bread, as in the photo. Put a slice of ham between the two slices of bread and grill, pressing the two pieces of bread together so that they are compact and stick together.

MORCILLA EN HOJA DE BERZA

BLACK PUDDING IN CABBAGE LEAVES

Ingredients: *Black pudding and cabbage.*

Method: Select a number of different types of onion black pudding and remove the fat by boiling them. Remove the skin from the black puddings and mix them together. Wrap in a boiled cabbage leaf and serve hot.

VOLOVÁN DE MANOS DE CERDO

PIGS' TROTTERS VOL-AU-VENTS

Ingredients: *Vol-au-vent cases, boiled and boned pigs' trotters, mushrooms, small "Padron" green peppers and "Burgundy" sauce.*

Method: Cut the mushrooms and peppers into julienne strips. Gently fry the mushrooms with the garlic, parsley and white wine. Gently fry the peppers in oil separately. Chop the pigs' trotters and mix with the peppers, mushrooms and "Burgundy" sauce. Fill the vol-au-vent cases with this mixture and serve hot.

CRÊPE DE BACALAO
AJOARRIERO

QUESO CON ANCHOAS
Y PIQUILLOS

PIMIENTO RELLENO
DE MEJILLÓN

CRÊPE DE BACALAO AJOARRIERO

COD PANCAKES A LA "AJOARRIERO"

Ingredients: *Pancakes, cod, red and green peppers, garlic, onion, white wine and Biscay sauce (dried spice pepper, onion and garlic).*

Method: Make the pancakes in the usual way. Prepare the "ajoarriero" with the desalted cod and the rest of the ingredients. Then add some "fumet"(strong fish stock) and the Biscay sauce. Stuff the pancakes with the cod mixture and arrange on a plate with the Biscay sauce as a base. Serve hot.

QUESO CON ANCHOAS Y PIQUILLOS

CHEESE WITH ANCHOVIES AND "PIQUILLO" PEPPERS

Ingredients: *Cheese spread, anchovies in oil, "piquillo" peppers, cream and brandy.*

Method: Finely chop the anchovies and peppers. Mix all the ingredients together and spread onto a slice of toasted bread. Serve at room temperature.

PIMIENTO RELLENO DE MEJILLÓN

PEPPERS STUFFED WITH MUSSELS

Ingredients: *"Piquillo" peppers, mussels, onion, green pepper, carrot, tomato, white wine, flour and milk.*

Method: Steam the mussels open and then chop them into small pieces. Gently fry the vegetables in oil and add the flour, white wine and tomato to make a bechamel sauce. Add the chopped mussels. Stuff the peppers with the mussel mixture and serve hot.

TARTALETA DE
PUERROS
ROLLITO DE
SALMÓN
TORTILLA
RELLENA

MANHATTAN

Plaza Zaragoza nº 3 • Tel.:943-46 45 10

TARTALETA DE PUERROS

LEEK TARTLETS

Ingredients: *I kg of leeks, flour, milk, cream, onion, prawns, pastry cases and white wine.*

Method: Gently fry the leeks in butter and oil. Add a little finely chopped onion; then a little white wine and water. Allow to boil thoroughly and then add the peeled prawns. Make a light bechamel sauce with the milk, flour and a little cream. Mix well. Fill the pastry cases and garnish with some prawns.

ROLLITO DE SALMÓN

SALMON ROLLS

Ingredients: *4 slices of smoked salmon, two crab sticks, half a chopped hard-boiled egg, chopped onion, mayonnaise, sliced bread and butter.*

Method: Chop the two crab sticks, half a hard-boiled egg, an onion and a little salmon. Add a little mayonnaise to form a paste, which is then rolled into the slices of salmon and arranged on squares of lightly buttered sliced bread.

TORTILLA RELLENA

STUFFED OMELETTE

Ingredients: *4 potatoes, onion, tuna fish, eggs, mayonnaise, tabasco sauce, mixed herbs.*

Method: Make two normal potato omelettes. Prepare a spread with chopped tuna fish, a hard-boiled egg and onion. Add mayonnaise and tabasco sauce to taste and a pinch of herbs. Mix well and spread between the two omelettes.

BONITO CON
ANCHOA
BACALAO
MEJILLONES
RELLENOS

BONITO CON ANCHOA

TUNA FISH WITH ANCHOVY

Ingredients: *Tuna fish, anchovies, hard-boiled egg, chopped onion, crab stick, mayonnaise and bread.*

Method: Chop the onion, egg and crab stick and flake the tuna fish. Mix thoroughly together with the mayonnaise and spread onto slices of fried bread. Garnish with an anchovy.

BACALAO

COD

Ingredients: *Desalted cod, onion, red pepper, green pepper and bread.*

Method: Cut 6 pieces of cod and dip into flour and egg. Fry in plenty of hot oil. Make a "ratatouille" with onion and peppers and cover the cod with it. Serve on a slice of bread.

MEJILLONES RELLENOS

STUFFED MUSSELS

Ingredients: *Mussels, cured ham, bechamel sauce, breadcrumbs and egg.*

Method: Clean and boil the mussels. Finely chop the mussels and ham. Prepare a bechamel sauce and add the mussels and ham. Fill the mussel shells with this mixture. Dip into egg and breadcrumbs and fry just before serving.

RELLENA DE
CREMA DE CENTOLLO

CHATKA RUSA

GELE DE
MOLLEJITAS D
PATO CON
VERDURAS

MARTÍNEZ

31 de Agosto nº 13 • Tel.:943-42 49 65

RELLENA DE CREMA DE CENTOLLO

SPIDER CRAB CREAM SPREAD

Ingredients: *200 g of white cheese spread, 100 g of spider crab meat, 2 salty anchovies and 3 courgettes.*

Method: Cut the courgette into thin slices and fry in plenty of oil. Drain on absorbent paper (kitchen roll). To make the cream beat the cheese, the spider crab meat and the anchovies together. Line a very small glass with the slices of courgette and fill with the cream mixture. Cover with more slices of courgette. Cool in the fridge for 15 minutes and then remove the cream from the glass as if it were a cream caramel. It can be served on a slice of toast.

CHATKA RUSA

RUSSIAN CHATKA

Ingredients: *200 g of Russian chatka (crab meat) and 1/4 litre of mayonnaise.*

Method: Flake the chatka taking care to remove any cartilage that might be present. Mix the two ingredients in a bowl. Cut some slices of bread and spread the mixture onto them.

GELE DE MOLLEJITAS DE PATO CON VERDURAS

DUCK GIZZARD WITH VEGETABLES IN ASPIC

Ingredients: *200 g of duck gizzards, 50 g of boiled ham, 6 large prawns, 3 button mushrooms, 1 courgette, spinach, runner beans, 3 sheets of fish gelatine, cream, meat stock and mayonnaise or potato puré.*

Method: Sauté the chopped vegetables and prawns in oil. Drain and chop further together with the gizzards. Soak the gelatine in cold water and whip the cream. Heat the stock and add the gelatine. Put the chopped ingredients in a bowl and add the gelatine and whipped cream and mix together slowly. Fill the moulds (glasses) with this mixture and chill in the fridge for an hour. Serve on a slice of toasted bread with mayonnaise or potato puré.

MOUSSE DE FO

MARÍA

MENFIS

Idiakez nº 6 • Tel.:943-42 80 74

DONOSTIARRA

DONOSTIARRA

Ingredients: *Toasted bread, fresh anchovies, "piquillo" red peppers, cured ham and truffled turkey ham .*

Method: Put a slice of cured ham onto the toasted bread. Take two cleaned anchovies and put a pepper and some turkey ham between them. Dip in flour and egg and fry in plenty of hot oil. Arrange on the ham and serve.

MOUSSE DE FOIE

LIVER PATE MOUSSE

Ingredients: *Liver pâté, kiwi fruit, mayonnaise, carrot, bilberries and pastry cases.*

Method: Make a liver pâté mousse with kiwi fruit and fill the pastry cases with it. Cover with a carrot mayonnaise (made by adding carrot juice to ordinary mayonnaise). On top of that put a slice of kiwi fruit and garnish with bilberry mayonnaise (made by adding bilberries to ordinary mayonnaise).

MARÍA

MARIA

Ingredients: *Sliced bread (containing currants, prunes and sweet chestnuts), truffled turkey ham, cured duck ham and cream cheese.*

Method: Cut a slice of the bread in half and fill with a slice of turkey ham. Spread some duck ham with cream cheese, make it into a roll and cut it into 3 pieces. Arrange on the bread as in the photo.

PINTXO DULCE
PREFERIDO
MENFIS

P I N T X O   D U L C E

SWEET PINTXO

Ingredients: *Rice tartlet cases, fruit in season: melon, apple, pear, banana. Gelatine.*

Method: This canape can be made with other fruit depending on the time of year. Fill a rice tartlet case with stewed fruit and decorate with different types of gelatine.

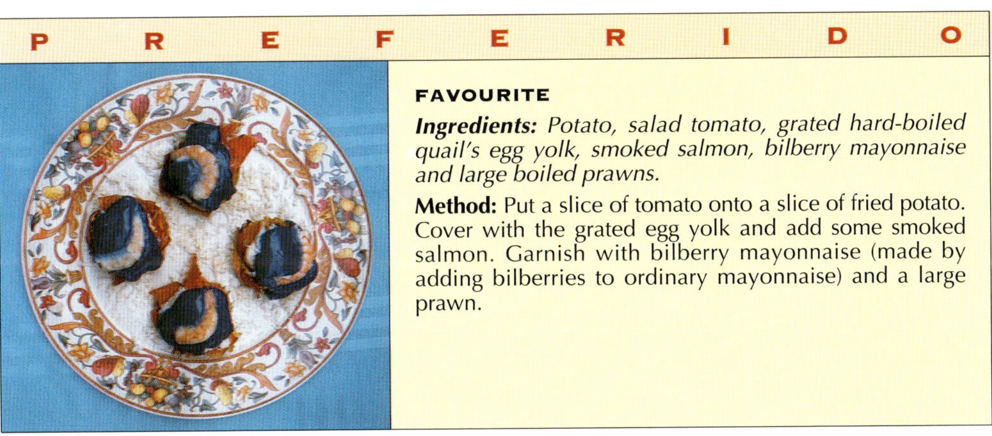

P R E F E R I D O

FAVOURITE

Ingredients: *Potato, salad tomato, grated hard-boiled quail's egg yolk, smoked salmon, bilberry mayonnaise and large boiled prawns.*

Method: Put a slice of tomato onto a slice of fried potato. Cover with the grated egg yolk and add some smoked salmon. Garnish with bilberry mayonnaise (made by adding bilberries to ordinary mayonnaise) and a large prawn.

M E N F I S

MENFIS

Ingredients: *Toasted bread, truffled turkey ham, roquefort cheese, green pepper and smoked anchovies.*

Method: Put the truffled turkey ham on a slice of toasted bread followed by the cheese and fried green pepper. Garnish with 2 smoked anchovies and grated hard-boiled egg white.

COCKTAIL
DE GAMBAS
GAMBAS
REBOZADAS
ENSALADA
DE POLLO

MOTO CLUB

Usandizaga nº 3 • Tel.: 943-28 41 54

COCKTAIL DE GAMBAS

PRAWN COCKTAIL

Ingredients: *Lettuce, crab sticks, boiled prawns, hard-boiled egg white and mayonnaise.*

Method: Chop all the ingredients and mix with the mayonnaise. Spread onto a slice of bread and garnish with a boiled, peeled prawn tail.

GAMBAS REBOZADAS

PRAWNS IN BATTER

Ingredients: *Peeled raw prawns, parsley, garlic, egg and flour.*

Method: Spear two prawns onto a cocktail stick, dip in flour and egg with chopped garlic and parsley. Fry in hot oil.

ENSALADA DE POLLO

CHICKEN SALAD

Ingredients: *Roast chicken breast, lettuce, green pepper, tomato and vinaigrette sauce.*

Method: Break up the chicken breast into small pieces and mix with the rest of the finely chopped ingredients. Garnish with cocktail sauce.

ATÚN
ANCHOA
SANDWICH
TARTALETA

ONDARRA

Avda. Zurriola nº 16 • Tel.: 943-27 09 92

ATÚN ANCHOA

TUNA FISH AND ANCHOVY

Ingredients: *Light tuna fish in oil, very finely chopped onion, mayonnaise, hard-boiled egg, sliced bread and anchovies in oil.*

Method: Cut the crusts off the bread and then cut each slice into 2 rectangles. Mix the tuna fish with the mayonnaise and spread on 1 rectangle of bread. Cover with the other rectangle. Garnish with grated hard-boiled egg and an anchovy.

SANDWICH

SANDWICH

Ingredients: *Sliced bread, red cabbage, curly endive (chicory), lettuce, tuna fish in oil, mayonnaise, oil and vinegar.*

Method: Mix the chopped red cabbage, endive, and lettuce with the mayonnaise. Add flaked tuna fish and spread onto some toasted bread. Cover to make a sandwich and cut into triangles.

TARTALETA

TARTLET

Ingredients: *Pastry cases, lettuce cut into thin strips, flaked tuna fish, chopped cheese slices, pieces of boiled ham, grated carrot, prawns, oil and vinegar.*

Method: Mix the tuna fish with the lettuce, cheese, ham and mayonnaise, which has been thinned with a little oil and vinegar. Fill the pastry cases with this mixture, and garnish with carrot and prawns, either whole or chopped.

RIÑONES

LECHERAS
DE TERNERA

O Ñ A T I

Miracruz nº 28B • Tel.: 943-28 26 15

GAMBAS A LA GABARDINA

PRAWNS IN BATTER

Ingredients: *Soda water, baking powder, salt, flour and prawns.*

Method: Put some soda water in a bowl, add baking powder, salt, flour and stir to form a paste. Coat the prawns with this mixture and fry in very hot oil.

RIÑONES

KIDNEYS

Ingredients: *Kidneys and bacon.*

Method: Chop the kidneys and remove all the fat. Fry the kidneys and bacon. Spear pieces of kidney and bacon alternately onto a cocktail stick until it is full.

LECHERAS DE TERNERA

CALVES' SWEETBREADS

Ingredients: *Sweetbreads, garlic and breacrumbs*

Method: Chop the sweetbreads, season them and add some very finely chopped garlic. Coat in breadcrumbs and fry in hot oil.

ORIENTAL
CHATKA
ANCHOAS

ORIENTAL

Miracruz nº 18 • Tel.: 943-29 03 03

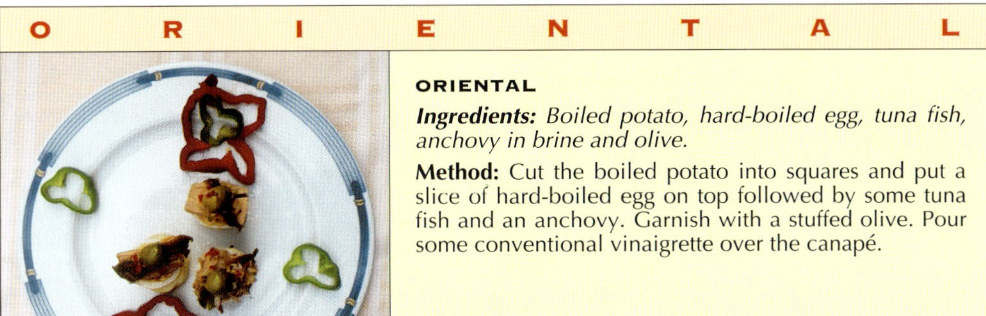

O R I E N T A L

ORIENTAL

Ingredients: *Boiled potato, hard-boiled egg, tuna fish, anchovy in brine and olive.*

Method: Cut the boiled potato into squares and put a slice of hard-boiled egg on top followed by some tuna fish and an anchovy. Garnish with a stuffed olive. Pour some conventional vinaigrette over the canapé.

C H A T K A

CRAB STICKS

Ingredients: *Crab sticks, boiled prawns, onion and pepper.*

Method: Cut the crab stick in half and spear each half onto a cocktail stick. Put a peeled prawn onto each end. Make a vinaigrette with the onion and pepper and cover the canapé with it.

A N C H O A S

ANCHOVIES

Ingredients: *Toasted bread, boiled ham, anchovies in brine, hard-boiled egg and mayonnaise.*

Method: Toast the bread and put some strips of boiled ham on it. Put a slice of hard-boiled egg on top. Garnish with mayonnaise, 2 anchoves and a little chopped hard-boiled egg.

CALABACÍN RELLENO

CÓCTEL DE CIGALITAS Y GAMBAS

REVUELTO DE NÍSCALOS

OROIPEN

Segundo Izpizua nº 16 • Tel.: 943-29 18 86

CALABACÍN RELLENO

STUFFED COURGETTE

Ingredients: *Courgette, cured ham, hard-boiled egg, green and red peppers and cherry tomatoes.*

Method: Cut the courgette into very thin slices. Put some cured ham, hard-boiled egg, red and green pepper between two slices. Dip in flour and egg and fry. Garnish with cherry tomatoes and raw peppers.

CÓCTEL DE CIGALITAS Y GAMBAS

NORWAY LOBSTER AND PRAWN COCKTAIL

Ingredients: *Small or large prawns, little Norway lobsters, eggs, oil and avocado pear.*

Method: Fry and chop the Norway lobsters. Boil and chop the prawns. Dress with a light mayonnaise made with avocado pear, and fill some vol-au-vent cases with this mixture.

REVUELTO DE NÍSCALOS

CHANTERELLE MUSHROOMS WITH EGG

Ingredients: *Chanterelle mushrooms, spring onion, garlic and quail's egg.*

Method: Finely chop and gently fry the onion and garlic. Add the chopped mushrooms and allow to cook. Put onto a piece of bread and garnish with hard-boiled quails' eggs and peppers.

PAVO
COMBINADO

BACON
AHUMADO

OSTARTE

Marina nº 8 • Tel.: 943-45 36 74

PAVO COMBINADO

TURKEY COMBINATION

Ingredients: *Turkey fillets, green peppers, oyster mushrooms and bread.*

Method: Coat the turkey fillets in flour, egg and breadcrumbs and fry along with the green peppers. Fry the mushrooms. Arrange on a piece of bread in the following order: peeled green pepper, turkey and finally the mushrooms.

REVUELTO DE HONGOS

EDIBLE FUNGI IN EGG

Ingredients: *Edible fungi, onion, young garlic shoots, egg and bread.*

Method: Chop the fungi and toss in oil with a little onion and some garlic shoots. Season and mix with the beaten eggs. Make scrambled egg with this mixture in a hot frying-pan. Serve on a slice of bread.

BACON AHUMADO

SMOKED BACON

Ingredients: *Courgette or aubergine, bacon, "piquillo" pepper, onion and bread.*

Method: Coat the courgette in flour and egg and fry in plenty of hot oil. Fry the bacon and pepper separately and cut them into strips. Fry some onion rings done in egg and breadcrumbs and arrange the ingredients on the piece of bread in this order: courgette, bacon, pepper and onion rings.

CHAMPIÑÓN
RELLENO
PIMIENTO
RELLENO DE
MORCILLA
PIMIENTO VERDE
RELLENO DE
CHIPIRÓN

CHAMPIÑÓN RELLENO

STUFFED MUSHROOM

Ingredients: *Button mushrooms, onion, red and green peppers, beef, turkey or fish, some bechamel sauce, breadcrumbs and egg.*

Method: On a low heat gently cook the mushroom stalks and finely chopped vegetables along with the beef or turkey or fish. The idea is to make a delicious paste to fill the mushroom caps. When this has been done dip the mushrooms in a bechamel sauce and breadcrumbs. Fry in plenty of oil and serve hot.

PIMIENTO RELLENO DE MORCILLA

PEPPERS STUFFED WITH BLACK PUDDING

Ingredients: *Black pudding, red "piquillo" peppers, garlic and oil.*

Method: Fry the black pudding and remove all the contents from the skin. Gently fry some peppers and fill them with the black pudding. Make a sauce with garlic, peppers and milk and strain it. Pour this sauce over the peppers.

PIMIENTO VERDE RELLENO DE CHIPIRÓN

GREEN PEPPERS STUFFED WITH SQUID

Ingredients: *Green peppers, squid, onion, tomato, squid ink, eggs, flour and hard-boiled egg.*

Method: Chop the squid and cook with a little onion and green pepper. Use this mixture to stuff the green peppers once they have been cooked. Dip in flour and egg and fry. Make a squid sauce in the same way as when preparing squid in ink. Pour the sauce over the peppers and garnish with grated hard-boiled egg.

TXALUPAS
DE ATÚN

BROCHETA
DE CHAMPIS

TORTILLA
OTZARAN

OTZARAN

Doctor Claudio Delgado nº 1 • Tel.: 943-29 11 53

TXALUPAS DE ATÚN

TUNA FISH BOATS

Ingredients: *Flaked tuna fish, chili peppers, "piquillo" red peppers and anchovy.*

Method: Put some tuna fish onto some crispbread with two pieces of chili pepper at each end. Then add the red pepper and anchovy fillet.

BROCHETA DE CHAMPIS

MUSHROOM KEBAB

Ingredients: *Button mushrooms, green pepper, bacon and salt.*

Method: Take a kebab stick and spear all the ingredients onto it alternately. Season and grill with a little oil.

TORTILLA OTZARAN

OTZARAN OMELETTE

Ingredients: *Potatoes, eggs, lettuce, tomato, mayonnaise, tuna fish and anchovies.*

Method: For the base make a potato omelette in the traditional way. Allow to cook and slice it across the middle. Spread on some mayonnaise together with the lettuce, tomato, tuna fish and anchovies.

COCKTAIL DE MARISCO

ENSALADA DE VERANO

ENSALADA DE SALMÓN

PACO BUENO

Mayor nº • Tel.: 943-42 49 59

COCKTAIL DE MARISCO

SEAFOOD COCKTAIL

Ingredients: *Boiled prawns, boiled Norway lobsters, tomato sauce, crab sticks, green pepper, gherkin, cocktail sauce and toasted bread.*

Method: Chop all the ingredients, mix with the cocktail sauce and spread onto the bread. Garnish with a boiled prawn or other seafood, if desired.

ENSALADA DE VERANO

SUMMER SALAD

Ingredients: *Tomato, tuna fish in oil, hard-boiled egg, boiled prawn, boiled potato, onion, parsley, oil and vinegar.*

Method: Spear all the ingredients onto a cocktail stick with the tomato and potato together at the bottom. Dress with a vinaigrette made of onion, parsley, oil and vinegar.

ENSALADA DE SALMÓN

SALMON SALAD

Ingredients: *Smoked salmon, boiled prawn, asparagus, olives and vinaigrette (onion, parsley, oil and vinegar).*

Method: Make a roll with a slice of smoked salmon and spear onto a cocktail stick together with the prawn, the asparagus and the olive. Dress with the vinaigrette.

CHAMPIÑONES RELLENOS

PIMIENTO CON ANCHOAS

PINTXO SUSO

PATA NEGRA

Isabel II nº 15 • Tel.: 943-45 01 47

CHAMPIÑONES RELLENOS

STUFFED MUSHROOMS

Ingredients: *Button mushrooms, onion, green pepper, breadcrumbs, mince meat, flour and egg.*

Method: Boil the mushrooms. Chop the onion and pepper and fry gently. Add the meat and breadcrumbs and fill the mushroom. Dip in flour and egg and fry. If desired, garnish with strips of green and/or red pepper.

PIMIENTO CON ANCHOAS

PEPPER WITH ANCHOVIES

Ingredients: *"Piquillo" red peppers, anchovies in oil and vinaigrette.*

Method: Cut a slice of bread and put a grilled pepper on top. Put some anchovy fillets on the pepper and dress with the vinaigrette.

PINTXO SUSO

SUSO PINTXO

Ingredients: *Lettuce, cocktail sauce, 4 prawns, strip of green or red pepper and hard-boiled egg.*

Method: Put a lettuce leaf on a slice of bread followed by some hard-boiled egg. Pour some cocktail sauce over everything. Arrange 4 boiled prawns on the sauce and garnish with a strip of red or green pepper.

LANGOSTINOS
CON BECHAMEL
CROQUETAS
DE OCA
CROQUETAS
DE MARISCO

RECALDE

Aldamar nº 1 • Tel.: 943-42 09 68

LANGOSTINOS CON BECHAMEL

LARGE PRAWNS WITH BECHAMEL SAUCE

Ingredients: *1 kg of large prawns, 3 tablespoonfulls of flour, 1 litre of milk, butter, egg and breadcrumbs.*

Method: Boil the prawns in water with salt. Peel and spear 2 of them onto a cocktail stick. Make a bechamel sauce with the butter (130 g), the flour and the milk and season. Coat the prawns in the bechamel sauce. Allow to cool. Dip into egg and breadcrumbs and fry.

CROQUETAS DE OCA

GOOSE CROQUETTES

Ingredients: *Goose meat, 3 tablespoonfulls of flour, 130 g of butter, a litre of milk, salt and pepper.*

Method: Finely chop the goose meat. Make a bechamel sauce with the flour, butter and milk. Mix with enough goose meat until the sauce takes on the colour of cream. Dip in egg and breadcrumbs and fry.

CROQUETAS DE MARISCO

SEAFOOD CROQUETTES

Ingredients: *Seafood: prawns, mussels, scallops, edible fungi or mushrooms (according to season) and monkfish. Paste: 3 tablespoonfulls of flour, butter and a litre of milk. Shallots, white wine and pepper.*

Method: Boil the prawns and steam the mussels open. Cook the scallops in butter with shallots, salt, pepper and white wine. When cooked add the diced monkfish. Cook the fungi separately and then mix with the scallops and monkfish mixture. Blend with a high-speed whisk. Make a bechamel sauce with the milk and some of the shellfish stock. Mix the bechamel sauce with the rest of the ingredients, dip in flour, egg and breadcrumbs and fry.

ANCHOA RELLENA

CHAMPIS CON JAMÓN

R I C A R D O

Gral. Artetxe nº 6 • Tel.: 943-27 05 61

A N C H O A   R E L L E N A

STUFFED ANCHOVIES

Ingredients: *Anchovies, salt, "piquillo" red pepper, flour, egg and oil.*

Method: Clean the anchovies and remove the bones. Take an anchovy, put half a cooked pepper on it, and cover with another anchovy. Season. Dip in flour and then egg and fry in hot oil.

G A M B A   R E B O Z A D A

PRAWN IN BATTER

Ingredients: *Prawn, salt, flour, egg, oil and fried bread.*

Method: Peel the prawns, season, dip in flour and egg and fry. Serve on fried bread.

C H A M P I S   C O N   J A M Ó N

MUSHROOMS WITH HAM

Ingredients: *Button mushrooms, onion, green pepper, garlic, chili pepper, cured ham, oil and tomato.*

Method: Chop the ingredients and fry gently. Add the mushrooms and ham. Season and add some tomato and white wine. Add some water and cook for about 20 minutes.

PERRITO

QUESO CON NUECES

BONITO A LO ROBERTO

ROBERTO

Gral. Artetxe nº 2 • Tel.: 943-27 40 96

PERRITO

HOT DOG

Ingredients: *Frankfurter sausage and bread roll.*

Method: Remove the inside of the bread roll and put a grilled frankfurter inside. Serve hot.

QUESO CON NUECES

CHEESE WITH WALNUTS

Ingredients: *Walnuts, cheese spread and bread.*

Method: Spread the cheese on the bread and garnish with walnuts.

BONITO A LO ROBERTO

ROBERTO'S TUNA FISH

Ingredients: *Tuna fish, olives, red and green pepper, onion, garlic, oil and vinegar.*

Method: Spear some pickled tuna fish and an olive onto a cocktail stick. Cover with a vinaigrette made with the rest of the ingredients.

JOHANA

BACALAO A LO SAYOA

PINTXO PELI

S A Y O A

Egia nº 1 • Tel.: 943-27 13 52

J O H A N A

JOHANA

Ingredients: *Small squid, onion, garlic, green peppers, small pastry cases, "fumet" (concentrated fish stock), potato puré, white wine and olive oil.*

Method: Clean and chop the squid and put the ink sacks in a glass with some water. Gently cook the vegetables in an earthenware dish. Brown the squid in a frying pan and add the vegetables. Add a glass of white wine to the juices the squid have released. Allow the liquid to evaporate a little. Then pour everything back into the earthenware dish. Add a cup of hot "fumet" and the squid ink. Allow to cook for a while and serve in the little pastry cases.

B A C A L A O A L O S A Y O A

COD A LA SAYOA

Ingredients: *Desalted cod, green peppers, onion, garlic, chili peppers, cayenne pepper and olive oil.*

Method: Chop the peppers and the onion into thin julienne strips and the garlic into slices and allow everything to fry gently on a low heat in a fair amount of oil. Cook the cod in an earthenware dish and when it is almost cooked add the vegetables and cayenne pepper. Allow the fish to cook completely for an instant and serve hot.

P I N T X O P E L I

PELI PINTXO

Ingredients: *Mussels, leeks, tomato, carrot, onion, garlic, Port, white pepper, butter, small pastry cases and olive oil.*

Method: Chop the leeks, carrots, onion, garlic and tomato and fry in an earthenware dish in very hot butter and oil. When they are almost cooked, add a glass of port, the pepper and the mussels. When everything is cooked, serve in the pastry cases.

PIQUILLOS RELLENOS
DE CHATKA

PASTEL DE
ESPÁRRAGOS
Y SALMÓN

PUDÍN DE KRABARROKA

ROCK-FISH PUDDING

Ingredients: *Rock fish, eggs, tomato, pepper, cream, quail's egg, prawn and mayonnaise.*

Method: Beat the eggs with the cream and tomato. Add the flaked rock fish and pepper. Mix well and pour into an oven mould greased with butter. Cook in the oven bain marie until it becomes firm. Cool and cut into slices. Garnish with a boiled quail's egg, a boiled, peeled prawn and mayonnaise. Serve on a slice of bread.

PIQUILLOS RELLENOS DE CHATKA

"PIQUILLO" PEPPERS STUFFED WITH CRAB STICKS

Ingredients: *"Piquillo" peppers, crab stick, hard-boiled egg, mayonnaise and bread.*

Method: *Chop the crab stick, one pepper and a hard-boiled egg and mix together with the mayonnaise. Stuff the pepppers with this mixture and serve on a slice of bread.*

PASTEL DE ESPÁRRAGOS Y SALMÓN

ASPARAGUS AND SALMON TARTS

Ingredients: *Asparagus, eggs, evaporated milk, smoked salmon, boiled prawns, cherry tomatoes and pastry tartlet cases.*

Method: Beat the eggs with the evaporated milk and add the chopped asparagus. Cook in the oven for about half an hour bain marie. Serve in a pastry tartlet and garnish with smoked salmon, a prawn and a cherry tomato.

TORTILLA DE BACALAO

ANCHOAS A LA MARINADA

CHORICILLOS COCIDOS

S O R G I Ñ A

Dr. Claudio Delgado nº 4 • Tel.: 943-27 94 89

A N C H O A S   A   L A   M A R I N A D A

MARINADED ANCHOVIES

Ingredients: *For 10 canapés: 1/2 kg of fresh anchovies, 1 tablespoonful of sea salt, a small glass of vinegar, an onion, a green pepper and stuffed olives.*

Method: Clean the anchovies, put them in a container with the salt and leave in the fridge for 24 hours. Afterwards, rinse them with water and cut them into fillets. Put them in a container with the vinegar and allow to marinade for 2 hours. Spear a number of fillets onto a cocktail stick ending with a stuffed olive. Garnish with some thin slices of pepper and onion and sprinkle with some olive oil.

T O R T I L L A   D E   B A C A L A O

COD OMELETTE

Ingredients: *For 10 canapés: 250 g of desalted cod, a large onion, 3 green peppers, 8 eggs and olive oil.*

Method: Finely chop the peppers and onion and gently fry in a saucepan with oil. When they are thoroughly softened add the flaked cod and allow everything to boil for about 2 or 3 minutes. Beat the eggs and add salt. Make an omelette with all these ingredients ensuring that it remains very moist. Serve on a slice of bread.

C H O R I C I L L O S   C O C I D O S

BOILED "CHORIZO" SAUSAGES

Ingredients: *"Chorizo" sausages from La Rioja, white wine, a meat stock cube and water.*

Method: Bring water with a stock cube and a little white wine to the boil. Add the sausages, lower the heat and allow them to boil gently for 45 minutes. Serve on a slice of bread or in French bread sandwiches.

CHAMPIÑÓN
TAMBORIL
MOUSSE DE
QUESO
ENSALADA
DE TXANGURRO

TAMBORIL

Pescadería nº 2 • Tel.: 943-42 35 07

CHAMPIÑÓN TAMBORIL

TAMBORIL MUSHROOM

Ingredients: *Button mushrooms, garlic, chili peppers, salt, olive oil, water and parsley.*

Method: In an earthenware dish bring to the boil a mixture of half water to half olive oil. Add lots of garlic and a pinch of parsley. Boil the mushrooms and chili pepper in this liquid for about 5-10 minutes. Allow to stand a little before serving.

MOUSSE DE QUESO

CHEESE MOUSSE

Ingredients: *Goat's milk cheese, roquefort cheese and milk.*

Method: Mix the cheeses together in an earthenware dish and add some milk. Bring to the boil and beat all the ingredients together. Allow to stand. Serve with toasted bread, in pastry cases or with biscuits.

ENSALADA DE TXANGURRO

SPIDER CRAB SALAD

Ingredients: *Spider crab meat, lettuce hearts, onion, mayonnaise and tabasco sauce.*

Method: Chop the lettuce hearts and onion and mix with the crab meat. Add mayonnaise and tabasco sauce and mix everything thoroughly.

PIMIENTO RELLENO

PASTEL DE PIMIENTO

GAMBAS CON BACON

TAMBORRAS

Matía nº 38 • Tel.: 943-21 73 91

PIMIENTO RELLENO

STUFFED PEPPER

Ingredients: *"Piquillo" red pepper, crab stick, large prawn, mayonnaise.*

Method: Chop the crab stick and prawn and mix with the mayonnaise. Stuff the pepper with this mixture and decorate with mayonnaise.

PASTEL DE PIMIENTO

PEPPER PUDDING

Ingredients: *Onion, leek, carrot, "piquillo" pepper, eggs, cream and tomato.*

Method: Chop the leek, onion and carrot and gently fry. Add tomato and the pepper. In a separate bowl beat the eggs, add the cream and fried vegetables and mix well. Pour into a mould and cook bain marie until firm.

GAMBAS CON BACON

PRAWNS WITH BACON

Ingredients: *Prawns and bacon.*

Method: Peel the prawns, roll in a slice of bacon, hold together with a cocktail stick and fry in hot oil.

ESPÁRRAGO RELLENO DE TXANGURRO

PUDING DE BACALAO

FOIE CON MOUSSE DE PIQUILLO

TABERNA BARÚN

Pescadores de Terranova nº 1 • Tel.: 943-46 56 04

ESPÁRRAGO RELLENO DE TXANGURRO

ASPARAGUS FILLED WITH SPIDER CRAB

Ingredients: *Thick asparagus, spider crab, "txakoli"(dry white Basque wine), tomato sauce, hard-boiled egg, brandy, margarine, oil, white pepper and salt.*

Method: Boil and flake the spider crab. Heat a little oil and add the spider crab, chopped hard-boiled egg, a little tomato sauce, margarine, "txakoli", brandy, white pepper and salt. Cut the asparagus down the middle and fill with the spider crab mixture. Dip in flour and egg and fry in very hot oil.

PUDING DE BACALAO

COD PUDDING

Ingredients: *"Piquillo" red pepper, green pepper, 200 g of cream, 8 eggs, white pepper, cod (300 g) and onion.*

Method: Chop the cod with the green peppers and onion and fry gently. Line a mould with butter and put some fried green peppers in the bottom of it. Then put a layer of the cod mixture and cover with the "piquillo" peppers. Finally add a mixture of eggs beaten with cream, salt and pepper and bake for 25 minutes at a medium heat.

FOIE CON MOUSEE DE PIQUILLO

PATE WITH "PIQUILLO" PEPPER MOUSSE

Ingredients: *Liver pâté, "piquillo" peppers, asparagus and mayonnaise.*

Method: Put a slice of liver pâté onto a rusk or slice of crispbread and cover with a mousse made of peppers beaten with mayonnaise. Garnish with a green asparagus tip.

CALAMARES

ROMPEPECHOS

ALCACHO
TENDIDO

TENDIDO CINCO

Secundino Esnaola nº 38 • Tel.: 943-27 60 40

CALAMARES

SQUID

Ingredients: *For the amount as shown in the photo: 100g of fresh squid, flour, a little baking powder, salt and soda water.*

Method: Clean the squid thoroughly and cut into strips. Make a batter with the rest of the ingredients, not forgetting the dash of soda water to make it lighter. Put the strips of squid in the batter after it has risen (about 20 mins). Mix well and cook in a deep frier at 180° until golden brown.

ROMPEPECHOS

ROMPEPECHOS

Ingredients: *1 tin of "piquillo" red peppers, garlic, salt, a little oil, a slice of fried bread and 14 fillets of anchovies in oil.*

Method: Fry the bread and allow to cool. Chop the peppers and anchovy fillets and mix together well. Drain if there is a lot of liquid. Spread some of the mixture on the bread. Garnish with an olive or a slice of gherkin.

ALCACHOFA TENDIDO 5

ARTICHOKE "TENDIDO 5"

Ingredients: *6 asparagus tips, 6 artichokes, 6 thin slices of cured ham, flour and egg.*

Method: Fry the asparagus and artichokes in flour and egg at a temperature of 200°. Wrap in a slice of ham. Spear onto a cocktail stick to hold everything together, and serve.

TEOREMA
ZABALETA
KONTXI

TEOREMA

Zabaleta nº 1 • Tel.: 943-29 36 12

T E O R E M A

TEOREMA

Ingredients: *Quail's egg, Iberian cured ham, smoked salmon, pastry tartlet case and mayonnaise.*

Method: Put some ham and smoked salmon mixed together with mayonnaise in a pastry case. Cover with a fried quail's egg.

Z A B A L E T A

ZABALETA

Ingredients: *Fried bread, mayonnaise, peas, potatoes, carrot, hard-boiled egg and large prawn.*

Method: Mix all the ingredients except the large prawn together. Spread onto a slice of bread and and put the prawn on top as a garnish.

K O N T X I

KONTXI

Ingredients: *Fried bread, fresh salmon, boiled potato, mayonnaise and parsley.*

Method: Marinade the salmon in oil for a few hours. Drain and arrange on a slice of bread. Put the potato on top followed by some mayonnaise and a sprig of parsley.

TARTALETA DE HONGOS

PRIMAVERA

PIMIENTO TIBURCIO

TIBURCIO

Fermin Calbeton nº 40 • Tel.: 943-42 31 30

TARTALETA DE HONGOS

EDIBLE FUNGI TARTLET

Ingredients: *Edible fungi, pastry, cream, prawns, garlic, salt and olive oil.*

Method: Bake the pastry tartlets. Toss the chopped fungi in olive oil with the garlic. Add white wine and cream and reduce the sauce. Fill the tartlets with this mixture and garnish with a boiled prawn.

PRIMAVERA

SPRING

Ingredients: *Bread, hard-boiled egg, boiled ham, crab stick, anchovy, mayonnaise and prawn.*

Method: Take a slice of bread and cover as follows: first a slice of ham, then a slice of hard-boiled egg, then the crab stick, after that an anchovy and a rosette of mayonnaise with a prawn on top to finish.

PIMIENTO TIBURCIO

TIBURCIO PEPPER

Ingredients: *Green pepper, Burgos cheese (ricotta), anchovy, fresh cheese spread and bread.*

Method: On a slice of bread put half a fried green pepper, then the Burgos cheese, an anchovy, and a nut of fresh cheese spread.

DEGUSTACIÓN
DE SALMÓN EN
CANAPÉ

DEGUSTACIÓN
DE CAVIAR EN
CANAPÉ

DEGUSTACIÓ
DE ROASTBEE
EN CANAPÉ

TOMÁS GROS

Corner of Miracruz & Tomás Gros • Tel.: 943-28 72 33

DEGUSTACIÓN DE SALMÓN EN CANAPÉ

SMOKED SALMON PINTXO

Ingredients: *Sliced bread, butter, lemon and smoked salmon.*

Method: Spread butter on the bread and put a very thin slice of smoked salmon on it. Sprinkle a little lemon juice on the salmon.

DEGUSTACIÓN DE CAVIAR EN CANAPÉ

CAVIAR PINTXO

Ingredients: *Sliced bread, butter, caviar, lemon and mayonnaise.*

Method: Spread butter on the bread and put some caviar on it. Sprinkle with lemon juice and garnish with mayonnaise.

DEGUSTACIÓN DE ROASTBEEF EN CANAPÉ

ROASTBEEF PINTXO

Ingredients: *Sliced bread, butter, beef entrecôte, gherkin in spicy sauce, spring onion, chili pepper, tomato, radish and mayonnaise.*

Method: Fry a quarter of a kilo of entrecôte in oil at 250°. When it is cooked, carve into very thin slices and wrap a gherkin in each slice. Put on a slice of buttered bread and garnish with the rest of the ingredients.

DONIBANEKO
HUEVO
RELLENO
PATÉ
CON ANCHOA

TRIKUA

Rue Padre Larroca

DONIBANEKO

DONIBANEKO

Ingredients: *Sliced bread, pickled tuna fish, mayonnaise sauce, anchovy, prawns and hard-boiled egg.*

Method: Remove the crusts from the bread and spread with the tuna fish mixed with the mayonnaise. Cover with another slice of bread and cut in half. At one end put a slice of hard-boiled egg with an anchovy fillet and mayonnaise and garnish with hard-boiled egg white. At the other end put a prawn with mayonnaise and garnish with hard-boiled egg yolk.

HUEVO RELLENO

STUFFED EGG

Ingredients: *Egg, tuna fish, mayonnaise, prawn and olive stuffed with anchovy.*

Method: Cut a hard-boiled egg in half and remove the yolk. Fill the space with some flaked tuna fish. Cover with mayonnaise and garnish with grated hard-boiled egg yolk. Garnish with a prawn and an olive on a cocktail stick stuck into the egg.

PATÉ CON ANCHOA

PATE WITH ANCHOVY

Ingredients: *Sliced bread, liver pâté and anchovy.*

Method: Toast the sliced bread and cut it into shape. Spread with the pâté and cover with anchovy fillets.

BOLA DE
CARNE
LENGUA
TXALINTXO

TXALINTXO

Segundo Izpizua nº 21 • Tel.:943-27 98 38

BOLA DE CARNE

MEAT BALL

Ingredients: *Flour, milk, butter, "piquillo" red pepper, mince meat, selection of vegetables and "Orly" batter.*

Method: Make a bechamel sauce (flour, milk and butter) and add the pepper, mince meat and vegetables, which have all been tossed in oil. Allow the mixture to cool and then roll it into balls. Dip in orly batter and fry in plenty of oil.

LENGUA

TONGUE

Ingredients: *Tongue, onion, leek, parsley, carrot. For the sauce: onion, leek, carrot, garlic, white wine, flour and the stock in which the tongue has been cooked.*

Method: Boil the tongue with the vegetables until it is tender. To make the sauce gently fry the vegetables, add some flour and fry gently until it changes colour slighty. Add white wine and stock and cook on a low heat. Strain.

TXALINTXO

TXALINTXO

Ingredients: *Pastry tartlet cases, vegetables in season, tomato sauce, brandy, mince meat, milk, flour and cream.*

Method: Fry the vegetables until cooked. Add flour and continue to cook. Then add the brandy, tomato sauce and milk. Bring to the boil and when cooked add some cream. Fill the pastry cases with this mixture and serve.

ANCHOAS CON PAPAYA

ANCHOAS CON ANCHOAS EN SALAZÓN

MONTADOS DE BACALAO AL AJO TOSTADO

TXEPETXA

Pescadería nº 5 • Tel.:943-42 22 27

ANCHOAS CON PAPAYA

ANCHOVIES WITH PAPAYA

Ingredients: *Anchovies, wine and cider vinegars, olive and sunflower seed oils, papaya in syrup and toasted bread.*

Method: Marinade the anchovies in the vinegars for about 3 hours. Fillet them and then soak them in the oils for 2 hours. Put two anchovy fillets on a slice of toasted bread and then a piece of papaya. Garnish with 2 mayonnaise rosettes.

ANCHOAS CON ANCHOAS EN SALAZÓN

FRESH AND SALTED ANCHOVIES

Ingredients: *Anchovies, wine and cider vinegars, olive and sunflour seed oils, salted anchovies, "piquillo" pepper and toasted bread.*

Method: On a base of toasted bread put two fillets of marinaded anchovy, followed by a fillet of salted anchovy and a strip of pepper. Garnish with finely chopped onion steeped in lemon juice.

MONTADOS DE BACALAO AL AJO TOSTADO

COD WITH GARLIC ON TOAST

Ingredients: *Flaked, desalted cod, garlic, onion, green pepper and toasted bread.*

Method: Finely chop plenty of onion and green pepper and fry gently for a long time on a very low heat with the flaked cod and conserve of garlic. To make the garlic conserve: take a large number of garlic cloves and without peeling them cook them on a very, very low heat for about 5 hours. Using a slice of toasted bread as the base, arrange a portion of cod cooked with the onion and pepper, and add some garlic conserve. Garnish with some mayonnaise made with the garlic conserve and brown under the grill for 4 minutes.

GILDAS

ANCHOAS
CON OLIVA

CHAMPI
AL HORNO

G I L D A S

GILDAS (CHILI PEPPERS)

Ingredients: *Chili peppers (tender and, if possible, from the coast), salted anchovies, stoned olives. These 3 ingredients must be of top quality.*

Method: Spear an anchovy fillet with 3 or 4 chili peppers (prepared in their vinegars) and the stoned olives onto a cocktail stick to make this "Gilda". (Perhaps it was in honour of the film character portrayed by Rita Hayworth; just as suggestive, spicy and beautiful!).

A N C H O A S   C O N   O L I V A

ANCHOVIES WITH OLIVE

Ingredients: *Anchovies, wine and cider vinegars, olive and sunflower seed oils, black olive paste and toasted bread.*

Method: Put two fillets of marinaded anchovies and a little black olive paste onto a slice of toasted bread. Garnish with a little finely chopped spring onion steeped in lemon.

C H A M P I   A L   H O R N O

BAKED MUSHROOMS

Ingredients: *Button mushrooms, green and red pepper, parsley, garlic, ham, tabasco sauce, oil and lemon.*

Method: Wash the mushrooms, finely chop everything else (peppers, parsley, garlic and ham) and fill the mushrooms with this mixture. Bake for 10 minutes and serve cut into pieces.

TXIKERO
MEJILLONES
RELLENOS
ANCHOAS
VINAGRETA

TXIKERO

José Arana nº 6 • Tel.:943-27 52 25

TXIKERO

TXIKERO

Ingredients: *Leek, onion, flaked cod, large prawns, egg and olive oil.*

Method: Cut the leek and onion into thin julienne strips and fry gently in oil on a low heat. Then add the cod and prawns. When everything has softened add the beaten egg and make a scrambled egg mixture. Serve on a slice of bread.

MEJILLONES RELLENOS

STUFFED MUSSELS

Ingredients: *Mussels, onion, red pepper, flour, milk, olive oil, egg, breadcrumbs and salt.*

Method: Gently fry the chopped mussel meat together with the chopped onion and pepper. Then make a bechamel sauce and add the cooked mussel, onion and pepper mixture. Fill the mussel shell with the sauce. Dip into beaten egg and breadcrumbs and fry in plenty of oil.

ANCHOAS VINAGRETA

ANCHOVIES IN VINAIGRETTE

Ingredients: *Anchovies, vinegar, olive oil, red and green pepper, onion and bread.*

Method: Marinade the cleaned anchovies in vinegar for 24 hours. Then rinse, season and put on a slice of bread. Cover with a vinaigrette made with vinegar, oil, peppers and onion.

BUÑUELOS
DE BONITO
PIMIENTO
DE TXANGURRO
MEJILLÓN CON
ESPINACA

TXIMISTA

Pl. de la Constitución nº 10 • Tel.:943-42 23 70

BUÑUELOS DE BONITO

TUNA FISH FRITTERS

Ingredients: *Tuna fish, boiled potato, onion, parsley and egg yolk.*

Method: Chop the potato, onion and parsley and flake the tuna fish. Mix with the egg yolk, roll the mixture into little croquettes and fry.

PIMIENTO DE TXANGURRO

PEPPERS WITH SPIDER CRAB

Ingredients: *Boiled spider crab, margarine, hard-boiled egg, tomato, white wine and "piquillo" peppers.*

Method: Flake the spider crab and chop the hard-boiled egg. Mix with the tomato and white wine. Stuff the peppers with this mixture.

MEJILLÓN CON ESPINACA

MUSSELS WITH SPINACH

Ingredients: *Mussels, tomato, bechamel sauce, spinach, eggs and breadcrumbs.*

Method: Boil the mussels. Prepare a bechamel sauce, finely chop the boiled mussels, boiled spinach, tomato, peppers, onion, garlic and hard-boiled egg and add to the sauce. Fill the mussel shells and fry in plenty of hot oil.

BONITO CON MAHONESA

CHAMPI A LA PLANCHA CON GAMBA

TXIRRITA

Isabel II nº 4 • Tel.:943-45 69 60

BONITO CON MAHONESA

TUNA FISH WITH MAYONNAISE

Ingredients: *Tuna fish in oil, onion, chili pepper and mayonnaise.*

Method: Flake the tuna fish and chop the onion and chili pepper very finely. Mix with the mayonnaise and spread onto a slice of bread.

CHAMPI A LA PLANCHA CON GAMBA

GRILLED MUSHROOMS WITH PRAWNS

Ingredients: *Button mushrooms, prawns and "ali-oli" garlic sauce (chopped garlic with parsley, oil and a little brandy).*

Method: Clean the mushrooms and grill with the prawns. When they are both cooked, pour some garlic sauce over them and serve.

BACALAO CON PIMIENTO VERDE

COD WITH GREEN PEPPER

Ingredients: *Desalted cod, green pepper and onion.*

Method: Cut the cod into pieces and fry with a little chopped green pepper and onion. Serve with the pepper and onion on top of the cod.

TARTALETA COCKTAIL

TXANGURRO

RAMIRO

TXOKO DE RAMIRO

Txofre nº 4 • Tel.:943-27 97 99

TARTALETA COCKTAIL

COCKTAIL TARTLET

Ingredients: *Pastry cases, large prawns, prawn cream, cocktail sauce and lettuce.*

Method: Boil and chop the large prawns. Add the prawn cream and cocktail sauce. Mix thoroughly and fill the pastry case, which already has a base of lettuce cut into thin julienne strips.

TXANGURRO

SPIDER CRAB

Ingredients: *Spider crab, spring onion, lettuce hearts from Tudela and crab cream.*

Method: Boil the spider crab and flake the meat. Chop the lettuce and onion very finely and mix with the spider crab. Add the cream of crab and a touch of tabasco sauce to taste. Serve in a pastry case or on a slice of toast.

RAMIRO

RAMIRO

Ingredients: *Cured Iberian ham, garlic, quails' eggs, mayonnaise and baked green pepper.*

Method: Make an "ali-oli" garlic sauce with the mayonnaise and garlic. Add the ham, hard-boiled quails' egg and green peppers, as shown in the photo.

HOJALDRE
DE BONITO

PUDÍN DE
MORCILLA

HOJALDRE DE BONITO

TUNA FISH IN PASTRY

Ingredients: *Vol-au-vent cases, tuna fish, egg, onion and fresh tomato.*

Method: Cook the tomato as for a "ratatouille" and allow to cool. Add the flaked tuna fish, and the finely chopped hard-boiled egg and onion. Mix thoroughly and fill the vol-au-vent cases with this mixture.

ANCHOAS CON PIMIENTO

ANCHOVIES WITH PEPPERS

Ingredients: *"Piquillo" red peppers, hot red Riojan chili pepper, and salty anchovies.*

Method: Put the anchovy fillets on a slice of bread and cover with the chopped pepper and hot chili pepper.

PUDÍN DE MORCILLA

BLACK PUDDING

Ingredients: *Black pudding (containing onion), vegetables, eggs and cream.*

Method: Mix all the ingredients together and pour into a pudding mould. Bake bain marie for an hour and a half.

ESPÁRRAGO
CON CHATKA

TARTALETA DE
ENSALADILLA

CABEZA DE JABALÍ

UDANE

Isabel II nº 6 • Tel.:943-45 14 01

ESPÁRRAGO CON CHATKA

ASPARAGUS WITH CRAB STICKS

Ingredients: *Fried bread, asparagus, crab sticks and vinaigrette made with onion, parsley and pepper.*

Method: Fry the bread and spread it with garlic. Put half an asparagus cut lengthwise on top. Add some crab stick and cover with the other half of the asparagus. Finally sprinkle with some vinaigrette made with dressed onion, parsley and pepper.

TARTALETA DE ENSALADILLA

POTATO SALAD TARTLET

Ingredients: *Pastry tartlet case, boiled potato, hard-boiled egg, prawns and mayonnaise.*

Method: Make a potato salad with all the ingredients and fill the pastry tartlet cases with it. Garnish with grated hard-boiled egg yolk and a prawn.

CABEZA DE JABALÍ

PIG'S BRAWN

Ingredients: *Toasted bread, pig's brawn, roquefort cheese and anchovies in oil.*

Method: Put a slice of the pig's brawn on the toast. Then put some roquefort cheese on top and garnish with an anchovy fillet.

GILDA UGARI

ENSALADA DE
VERDURA

VEGETAL "CORO"

U G A R I

Felipe IV nº 6 • Tel.:943-45 57 04

G I L D A U G A R I

UGARI CHILI PEPPERS

Ingredients: *Tuna fish, chili peppers, anchovies, olives and vinaigrette sauce (onion, red and green peppers, oil, vinegar and salt).*

Method: Spear some chili peppers onto a cocktail stick. Then add an olive, an anchovy and a piece of tuna fish. Dress with the vinaigrette sauce.

E N S A L A D A D E V E R D U R A

VEGETABLE SALAD

Ingredients: *Tomato, green pepper, tuna fish, mayonnaise, anchovy, hard-boiled egg and bread.*

Method: Chop the tomato, pepper and tuna fish and mix with the mayonnaise. Spread this mixture onto a slice of bread and garnish with an anchovy and grated hard-boiled egg.

V E G E T A L " C O R O "

"CORO" VEGETABLES

Ingredients: *Tomato, lettuce, hard-boiled egg, tuna fish, mayonnaise and bread.*

Method: Put a lettuce leaf onto a slice of bread. On top of that put a slice of tomato, a slice of hard-boiled egg some mayonnaise, and tuna fish. Sprinkle with grated hard-boiled egg.

URKABITO

POLLO VERDE

BACALAO GROS

URKABE

Segundo Izpizua nº 33 • Tel.:943-29 18 91

URKABITO

LITTLE URKABE

Ingredients: *Cod, pepper and onion. For the bechamel sauce: flour, butter, milk and salt.*

Method: Prepare a bechamel sauce and give it a distinctive flavour by adding a little fried onion and some of the juice from the fried cod. Fry the cod on a low heat. Cut into small portions so that it can be speared onto a cocktail stick together with the pepper. Dip the cod and pepper pieces in the bechamel, allow to cool, dip in flour, egg and breadcrumbs and fry.

POLLO VERDE

GREEN CHICKEN

Ingredients: *Chicken, lettuce and mayonnaise.*

Method: Fry some chicken breasts and flake the meat. Wash the lettuce thoroughly, chop it and let it dry. Make the mayonnaise with egg, lemon, oil, vinegar and salt. Mix everything together and spread onto a slice of bread.

BACALAO GROS

COD GROS STYLE

Ingredients: *Cod, "piquillo" pepper and mayonnaise.*

Method: Fry the cod with plenty of onion, a little garlic and some parsley. Make some mayonnaise with egg, lemon, oil, vinegar and salt. When the cod is cold, flake it. Cut the peppers into pieces. Mix these two ingredients together. Spread some mayonnaise onto a slice of bread and put the cod and pepper mixture on top.

PASTEL DE ANCHOAS

PIMIENTO RELLENO

URKIA

U R K I A

José Mª Salaberría nº 3 • Tel.:943-45 61 07

P A S T E L D E A N C H O A S

ANCHOVY CAKE

Ingredients: *Anchovy paste, cream, mayonnaise and toasted bread.*

Method: Make a thick spread by mixing the anchovy paste with the cream. Toast some thin slices of bread and spread on some of the anchovy and cream spread. Cover with a thin layer of mayonnaise.

P I M I E N T O R E L L E N O

STUFFED PEPPER

Ingredients: *"Piquillo" red peppers, mince meat, green and red pepper, parsley, onion and carrot.*

Method: Prepare the meat by frying it with a little garlic, onion and green pepper. Fill the red peppers with this mixture and cover with a sauce made of red pepper, carrot, onion and tomato.

U R K I A

URKIA

Ingredients: *Green pepper, tuna fish in oil, hard-boiled egg, toasted bread and mayonnaise.*

Method: Gently fry the green peppers and then prepare a mixture by flaking the tuna fish and adding some very finely chopped onion. Stuff the peppers with this mixture and then arrange them on the toasted bread and garnish according to taste.

PINTXO DE
TEMPORADA

MOUSSE DE
ESPÁRRAGO
TRIGUERO

BACALAO
AL PIL-PIL

U R O L A

Fermin Calbeton nº 20 • Tel.:943-42 34 24

PINTXO DE TEMPORADA

PINTXO OF THE SEASON

Ingredients: *Avocado pear, duck cured ham, Belgian endive, roquefort sauce and lettuce.*

Method: Spread some roquefort sauce onto the endive leaf followed by two slices of duck ham and two of avocado pear. Add a little lettuce and season with a little vinaigrette.

MOUSSE DE ESPÁRRAGO TRIGUERO

GREEN ASPARAGUS MOUSSE

Ingredients: *Green asparagus, smoked salmon and duck cured ham.*

Method: Arrange bands of different flavours of the asparagus and salmon onto a fairly thick mousse. Garnish with an asparagus tip and a small piece of duck cured ham.

BACALAO AL PIL-PIL

COD A LA PIL-PIL

Ingredients: *Cod, garlic, oil and pepper.*

Method: Gently cook the garlic, pepper in oil and add the cod in chunks. Cook only briefly. Serve with pieces of pepper on top.

TORTILLA DE BACALAO

ANCHOA EN SALAZÓN

JAMÓN Y LOMO DE SÁNCHEZ ROMERO

VALLÉS

Reyes Católicos nº 10 • Tel.:943-45 22 10

TORTILLA DE BACALAO

COD OMELETTE

Ingredients: *Cod, eggs, oil, onion and green pepper.*

Method: First gently fry the onion with the green pepper. Add the desalted cod. After a few minutes bind all this together with eggs beaten with parsley, to make a moist omelette. Serve in triangles.

ANCHOA EN SALAZÓN

SALTY ANCHOVIES

Ingredients: *Salted anchovies, oil, green pepper and onion.*

Method: First fry the green pepper and onion on a low heat. Then put a piece of green pepper followed by an anchovy onto a slice of bread. Garnish with fried onion and a piece of "piquillo" red pepper.

JAMÓN Y LOMO DE SÁNCHEZ ROMERO

SANCHEZ ROMERO CURED HAM & CURED LOIN OF PORK

Ingredients: *The secret of this exquisite food is to be found in the cured Iberico ham and loin of pork from the Sierra de Aracena, in the town of Jabugo (Huelva), where the animals are fed exclusively on acorns. The ham sandwich is the most popular snack. There cannot be anyone who hasn't eaten a ham sandwich at Vallés. This snack is popular at any time of the day.*

BACALAO
DE NICO

PIMIENTOS
CON GULAS

TARTALETA
DE LANGOS

V E R G A R A

Mayor nº 21 • Tel.:943-43 10 73

B A C A L A O   D E   N I C O

NICO'S COD

Ingredients: *Lightly smoked cod, fried onion and green peppers, rosemary vinegar and virgin olive oil.*

Method: Gently fry the onion and pepper and fill the cod slices with them.

P I M I E N T O S   C O N   G U L A S

PEPPERS WITH "GULAS"

Ingredients: *"Piquillo" red peppers from Mendavia or Lodosa, "gulas" (imitation elvers or baby eels), chili pepper, garlic, olive oil.*

Method: Gently heat the "gulas" together with the chili peppers and garlic in oil and use them to stuff the peppers.

T A R T A L E T A   D E   L A N G O S T A

LOBSTER TARTLETS

Ingredients: *Lobster tails, grated hard-boiled egg, tomato, nutmeg, white pepper, sage, oregano and pastry.*

Method: Make a "pudding" with all the ingredients. Flake and fill the pastry tartlets.

ANCHOAS
VITTORIO
MEJILLONES
RELLENOS
CESTITAS DE
BONITO

V I T T O R I O

Manterola nº 6 • Tel.:943-46 21 01

A N C H O A S   V I T T O R I O

VITTORIO ANCHOVIES

Ingredients: *Anchovies, onion, "piquillo" pepper, button mushrooms, flour, egg, oil and salt.*

Method: Clean the anchovies thoroughly and open them out. Finely chop the onion, peppers and mushrooms and fry them gently in oil in a frying pan. Fill the anchovies with this mixture. Dip the anchovies in flour and egg and fry. Serve on a slice of bread.

M E J I L L O N E S   R E L L E N O S

STUFFED MUSSELS

Ingredients: *Leeks, onion, carrot, mussels, monk fish, flour, milk, butter, oil and salt.*

Method: Clean the mussels and give them a quick boil. Remove the mussels from the shells and chop the mussel flesh. Clean and boil the monk fish. Gently fry the vegetables in another saucepan and when cooked, puré them. Put some butter in another saucepan and add the mussels, chopped monkfish and make a bechamel sauce with them. Then add the puréed vegetables and boil for a few minutes. All the mixture to cool and then fill the mussel shells with it. Dip them in flour and egg and fry.

C E S T I T A S   D E   B O N I T O

TUNA FISH BASKETS

Ingredients: *Tuna fish in oil, onion, tomato sauce, tartlet cases and prawns.*

Method: Chop the onion and add the drained and flaked tuna fish and tomato sauce. Mix everything together and fill the tartlet cases with this mixture. Garnish with a boiled peeled prawn.

BONITO
VERANIEGO
AUTÉNTICO

ZAGUÁN

31 de Agosto nº 28 • Tel.:943-42 48 44

BONITO

TUNA FISH

Ingredients: *Tuna fish, semi-blended tomato, "piquillo" pepper, onion, green pepper and anchovies in oil.*

Method: Flake the tuna fish and finely chop the "piquillo" pepper and onion. Mix everything thoroughly and add the tomato. Top with an anchovy fillet in oil and garnish with some finely chopped onion and green pepper.

VERANIEGO

SUMMERTIME

Ingredients: *Boiled potato, tuna fish, tomato, prawn, olive oil and vinegar.*

Method: Cut the potato to make a base which will form the base of the canapé. On top of the potato put a piece of tuna fish, a slice of tomato and a boiled prawn. Dress with oil and vinegar.

AUTÉNTICO

AUTHENTIC

Ingredients: *Mayonnaise, boiled ham, processed cheese, tuna fish, salad tomato and onion.*

Method: Chop the ham, cheese, and onion thinly and cut up the tomato. Mix together in a bowl and add the mayonnaise and tuna fish. This can be garnished with a boiled prawn or an anchovy in oil.

PULPO
ANCHOAS EN
VINAGRETA
VEGETAL
ZERUKO

ZERUKO

Pescadería nº 10

PULPO

OCTOPUS

Ingredients: *Octopus and paprika.*

Method: Boil and octopus and cut into pieces. Spear a number of pieces of octopus onto a coctail stick and sprinkle with paprika.

ANCHOAS EN VINAGRETA

ANCHOVIES IN VINAIGRETTE

Ingredients: *Fresh anchovies, vinegar, onion, green pepper and stuffed olives.*

Method: Clean the anchovies and marinade in vinegar for 24 hours. Then remove from the vinegar, spear onto a cocktail stick and cover with a vinaigrette made with green pepper, onion, oil and vinegar. Put a stuffed olive onto one end of the cocktail stick so as to hold everything together.

VEGETAL ZERUKO

ZERUKO VEGETABLE PINTXO

Ingredients: *Sliced bread, lettuce, tomato, cheese, tuna fish and mayonnaise.*

Method: Toast the sliced bread and make sandwiches of lettuce, tomato, cheese and tuna fish mixed with mayonnaise. Other ingredients can be added. Serve cut into triangles as shown in the photo.

BOLSA DE JUDAS

CESTITA DE ROQUEFORT

NIDO DE CODORNICE

ZULO-ZAHAR

Justo Elizarán nº 52 • Tel.:943-27 44 88

BOLSA DE JUDAS

JUDAS' MONEY BAG

Ingredients: *Spider crab, leeks, carrot, tomato, salt, oil and rice paper.*

Method: Boil the spider crab and allow to cool. Gently fry the leek and carrot in oil. When cooked, chop finely and add the spider crab. Put on a low heat and add one glass of plain tomato puré. Cook gently and season to taste. When cooked, put some of the mixture in a piece of rice paper and tie with a thin strip of leek. Bake in the oven until brown.

CESTITA DE ROQUEFORT

ROQUEFORT BASKET

Ingredients: *Potatoes, blue cheese and cream.*

Method: Beat the cheese with the cream. Make the potato basket in a mould and fill with the cheese mousse. Garnish with diced gherkin.

NIDO DE CODORNICES

QUAIL'S NEST

Ingredients: *Potato, leeks, carrots and quails.*

Method: Roast the quails with the chopped vegetables and allow to cool. Separate the meat from the bones and mix with the vegetables. Add cream, eggs and salt to taste. Cook, and put into the mould made of intertwined straw potatoes in the shape of a nest.

AHUMADOS

BACALAO CON VINAGRETA DE TOMATE

PASTEL DE SETAS

AHUMADOS

SMOKED SELECTION

Ingredients: *Butter, salmon, anchovies and hard-boiled egg.*

Method: Butter a slice of toast. Chop the salmon and put on one part of the slice of toast. Do the same with the anchovies, and garnish with chopped hard-boiled egg white down the middle of the canape.

BACALAO CON VINAGRETA DE TOMATE

COD WITH TOMATO VINAIGRETTE

Ingredients: *Cod, tomato, vinegar, salt and oil.*

Method: Desalt the cod and cook it very briefly. Break it up into flakes. Make a vinaigrette with diced tomato, vinegar and oil.

PASTEL DE SETAS

MUSHROOM CAKE

Ingredients: *Mushrooms, onion, cream, eggs, oil and salt.*

Method: Cook the mushrooms with the onion in the oven until brown. Then chop them. In a separate oven mould beat the cream and eggs. Add the chopped mushrooms and onions and bake bain marie. The accompanying sauce is made of cream and mushrooms.

INDEX